HOME AND SCHOOL: a child's-eye view

HOME AND SCHOOL:
a child's-eye view

Jacqueline Goodnow
Ailsa Burns

Macquarie University

WITHDRAWN

ALLEN & UNWIN
Sydney London Boston

To parents, teachers and all child-watchers

First published 1985
Allen & Unwin Australia Pty Ltd
8 Napier Street, North Sydney, NSW 2060, Australia

George Allen & Unwin (Publishers) Ltd
Park Lane, Hemel Hempstead, Herts HP2 4TE England

Allen & Unwin Inc.
Fifty Cross Street, Winchester, Mass 01890 USA

National Library of Australia
Cataloguing-in-Publication entry:

Goodnow, Jacqueline, 1924–   .
  Home and school.

  ISBN 0 86861 487 4.
  ISBN 0 86861 479 3 (pbk.).

  1. Children – Attitudes. 2. Children – Interviews.
  3. School children – Attitudes. 4. Family –
  Attitudes.   I. Burns, Ailsa.   II. Title.

305.2'3

Library of Congress Catalog Number: 85-70232

Set in 11/12.5pt English 49 by
Graphicraft Typesetters Ltd., Hong Kong
Printed in China by Bright Sun
(Shenzhen) Printing Co Ltd

ACKNOWLEDGMENTS

We are happy to acknowledge the help of several people. Some were officially research assistants but contributed insights beyond that role. Alphabetically, they are Lesley Dawes, Leonie Gilmour, Margaret Kennedy, Beth Spencer, Jacqueline Smith, and Ann Young. Beth Spencer and Lesley Dawes, in particular, contributed greatly to the general organisation and planning. Jan Bohan, with the assistance of Miriam Armstrong, patiently saw chapters through their several drafts; Graham Ryan kept essential track of finances. Bob Goodnow produced the charts. Final stages of the manuscript preparation were assisted by support from the Spencer Foundation while the senior author was a Fellow at the Center for Advanced Study in the Behavioral Sciences, Stanford. Of critical importance has been the role of the Department of Social Security, which financed this report and whose members initiated and implemented the survey from which we have drawn results.

CONTENTS

TABLES AND FIGURES

Tables

Figures

PREFACE

This book is for people interested in how children think and feel about the world around them: the world of family life, school, and friendships. They may be parents or teachers: they may have come to be child-watchers by profession or out of simple fascination.

This book is also for people who would prefer to have children use their own words to express their views, rather than always have some third party tell them about children. We have included as many verbatim statements as we can, and have built a framework from the comments rather than imposing a pre-existing theory upon them.

In the course of listening to the children's comments and noting the way they hang together, the reader will encounter a number of concepts about children and their environments. These concepts encompass the course of child development, and the way in which the settings of home and school, and the transitions they involve, match or disappoint the hopes and expectations children bring to them. They are also about the way children struggle to make sense of the world around them, and come to terms with it and finally, about how things could be improved: proposals for change that come partly from us, but mainly from the children themselves. Our goal has been to avoid having these ideas become dryly academic, instead letting them emerge from the children's statements.

It was not easy to set aside comments which we might have quoted, and to bring the others together in a way that said something new and avoided having the comments become just a list. The effort was sustained by the vividness and colour of the children's words and by the convictions that the least we could do was match the effort children put into making sense of their everyday life. To the children who supplied the spark, our thanks.

INTRODUCTION:
towards a new perspective

Children spend the major part of their day in two settings. What are their views of these settings and of the people in them? In this book we listen as children tell us what they see as the good and the not-so-good parts of home and school and of relationships with family members, teachers and friends: the joys, the hopes and expectations, the disappointments. They tell us also how they make sense of the world around them: what they find reasonable, what they find puzzling, what they perceive to be the underlying rules applying to various situations, and how they explain events and people's behaviour. And they tell us how home and school might be re-arranged, giving suggestions for keeping the best parts as well as suggestions for improvement.

We have tried to give as much space as possible to the children's own words. The comments come from 2000-odd primary school children in many parts of Australia, talking about such everyday concerns as getting started in the morning, jobs around the house, and what makes a good parent, teacher or friend. The children were happy to present their views. They also saw benefits to themselves and to adults in the process. In the words of some sixth-graders:

It makes a person feel good, that someone wants to listen.

Children know different things from the adults and times have changed. When adults were kids, things were different for kids from what they are now. Like, we have got disco now and when they were young, they had the waltz.

You have to talk and people have to listen. People can't read your mind and they can't see what you're thinking.

1

Children think of different things from adults, so adults can learn from kids' ideas.

We too see benefits in listening. The three main benefits in our eyes have to do with understanding children, understanding the contexts or settings in which they live, and understanding individual differences. All three are essential if we are to make good decisions for children and arrange good environments for them.

Understanding children

We often assume that we know what children are like. We know what they want, how they think, what matters to them, what is good for them. Very often we know less than we think.

One reason for this is that we see children and their lives through adult eyes. We interpret what they do and say using memories of our own past experiences as children even though, as the children note, 'times have changed'. We also use the images and pre-conceptions built into the conventional wisdom of our times. Throughout history, these images of children have shown some dazzling swings. Children have sometimes been perceived as vulnerable, tender vines and sometimes as tough plants that will burst through concrete, whose talent will 'out' in the worst of circumstances. They have sometimes been thought of as angels trailing clouds of glory, sometimes as imps of darkness, carrying a heavy burden of original sin and inevitably headed for mischief. For all that children often live up to expectations, it is not likely that the basic nature of children exhibits such radical changes. The major changes are in the prisms or filters that form the adult view.[1]

How can we be more flexible in our perceptions of children? One way is to consider some new ideas offered by psychologists. The image of 'children as novices' is an example. At various times, we are all novices: at parenting, at a new job, in a new city, or on retirement. Children are simply novices in more areas.[2] When they have the benefit of special experience—with computers, with a game such as chess, or with the rules of children's friendships— they may become the experts and emerge as more knowledgeable and skilled than adults.

We hope the comments quoted in this book and our additions to them will provide another route to changes in our image of

children. We have been impressed by how articulate and perceptive the children were, by how hard they work at trying to
understand their world, and by the significance to them of parts of
their lives that we might be tempted to set aside as minor features.
We are sure our readers will share this experience.

Understanding contexts

Adults are constantly amazed at the speed with which children
change and grow up. We see a world of difference between the
infant and the toddler, between the preschooler and the child in
the middle years of primary school. In our eyes, these changes all
come from within children, from maturational changes in their
capacity and from shifts in the knowledge they accumulate
through experience.

None of that development occurs in a vacuum, however. The
preschooler and the second-grader are different not only in age
and in their degree of experience. They are also living in different
settings or worlds, each with its own activities, demands, and casts
of characters. They may well appear to be such different people
because they live very different lives in different places: one is
largely a homebody, the other a member of a clamorous throng.

We are not likely to understand people unless we understand the
contexts in which they live and the way they encounter changes in
context. The psychologist who has made this point most forcefully
is Bronfenbrenner.[3] In his view, life consists of transitions between contexts or settings. People go back and forth between the
settings of home, school, workplace, shopping centre and other
places. Over time, a child moves from being a preschooler to being
a pupil in primary school, and then moves to one new grade after
another. There are moves from one home to another, or from one
set of friendships to another.

One way to understand children is to ask: What are these
transitions like? What makes some smooth, some bumpy, some
rewarding, some disappointing? How does it feel to change into
being a child at school, encountering new relationships with
teachers, with peers and perhaps a few bullies? What is it like to
move up to a new class, learning to cope with a new teacher, new
work and new classmates? What lies behind judgments such as
the following, offered by a second-grader: 'My new school is a

good school except when you get off the bus the boys throw rocks at you'?

In all such cases we also need to ask: What links does a child see between one setting and another? For example, children come to know what you can take from one setting to another. We can learn something from the words of two first-graders talking about school: while one said, 'I don't like school. You can't bring your parents or your pets with you', the other commented, 'I like school. I can bring my teddy bear'.

Children also come to know the steps you need to take in order to move from one setting to another, gaining the type of knowledge not yet acquired by a second-grader who commented: 'What do you do if you want to be a teacher? Do you just ask the teacher?'.

The nature of individual differences

While attempting to understand the general nature of children and the contexts in which they live, it is naturally important to also understand individual differences. Obviously, not all children have the same experience of school or of home. Often the differences between individual experiences are explained by classing some schools as privileged, some as disadvantaged, and others as isolated, as well as by categorising families as middle-class, working-class or upper-class.

We want to avoid such labels. The reasons are threefold. One is that the labels (and the stereotypes they imply) often do not fit with the way children perceive their own lives. Here, for instance, is a joyful description of life written by a third-grader in a 'disadvantaged' inner-city school:

> I wish I had a bike and a boat. I want the bike because I can go around my Aunty's house. I would like to live in a flat so I can stay up there and look down to see all the the small people looking back at me. I wish I had a cat. And I wish I stayed on the holiday to my Aunt's house. I like living there because they got a milk bar. We get all the chocklates and pies and a lot more stuff. I like going to the movies to see the rude ones. Once I went to the movies with my uncle's car. He stayed there with us too. I like going on picnics and play ther and catch yabbies. I like going to the beach and collecting some shells. I like catching some fish. I wish I had two dogs.

A similar discrepancy between the outsider's label and the child's view emerges in an exchange between an interviewer and a second-grader.

> INTERVIEWER: What are the faviourite things you like doing with your family?
> CHILD: Playing games with them, helping them . . . looking after daddy.
> INTERVIEWER: Is daddy sick?
> CHILD: Yes.
> INTERVIEWER: What's the matter?
> CHILD: Cancer. I play scrabble with him.

In conventional terms, this child's life is dramatically different from those of most children. What the child has done, however, is to weave the unusual event into the fabric of everyday life. The same interweaving occurs with the sixth-grader who wishes 'my brother were not handicap [*sic*] so there would not be so much of a rush in the morning'. In both cases, the dramatic or unusual in the adult's eyes is for the child part of the normal activities and relationships of everyday life.

A second reason for avoiding the usual labels is that we have come to feel that many issues cut across the usual social differences. The importance of friendships, of parents who have time to discuss things, of teachers who let you 'talk a little' in class or who take an occasional lesson 'outside'—these feelings appeared to be widely shared.

Finally, we have wanted to find some new ways of comparing children's lives. We wanted to locate basic differences that alter the way children feel or the way their daily life unfolds. By avoiding conventional labels, we feel that we can clarify, for example, the way in which certain transitions may open up new opportunities, or close off some options—or both.

Consider, say, a child who travels for two hours each morning and afternoon in order to attend a particular private school. In standard terms, she is 'advantaged'; the school is a 'good' one. From another point of view, she has been disadvantaged by the fact that a large part of her day has disappeared in travel. Rather than class this child as advantaged or disadvantaged, we have preferred to look at the way in which this transition has opened up some possibilities and limited others. Even the two-hour journey is not necessarily a disadvantage: this particular pupil travels a fair part of the distance by car with her father and her sister, and in her words, 'we get the chance to talk'. Considering the number of comments on the unavailability of fathers, this opportunity is a definite plus.

These general goals of understanding children and the contexts in which they live, as well as understanding their individual differences, provides the main framework for the way we shall analyse the children's comments.

The source of the children's comments

The voices in this book belong to children in primary schools scattered throughout Australia: they range from those in the centre of a city of four million people to those living on an island off the tropical coast of Darwin where you could walk to school 'except for the crocodiles'. The children talked at school in groups of six to eight, responding to questions asked by an adult inter- viewer. The adult controlled the discussion to the extent of obtaining an answer to each question from each child, but in no set order and with a tolerance for interesting detours. A few of the questions were given written answers by individual children. Most were discussed in the group and taped. What we and six student assistants have done is to read transcripts and listen to tapes, grouping comments and always asking: What are the children telling us about their lives?

Two discussion groups were set up in each of 145 schools. One group was drawn from the first three grades of primary school ('juniors'); the other from the latter three grades ('seniors'). Most of the groups contained children who were all from the same grade level (for example, Grade 5). A few contained a mixture of two grades (for example, Grades I and 2). With eight children in a group, the total sample was large: more than 2000 children. The schools were selected as a representative sample of schools by the Australian Bureau of Statistics. The choice of questions, the interviewing, and the transcribing of tapes were organised by the Department of Social Security. The result was a rich source of data that contains some specifically Australian touches, but may also be seen in a universal context.

How the children's views are presented

We shall use many verbatim statements, allowing the flavour of the children's comments to come through as fully as possible. In contrast we shall use numbers sparingly. Group discussions have the advantage of creating a situation where children are more likely to speak freely than when they are in a one-to-one interview with an adult. It does mean, however, that questions can come to be re-interpreted as the discussion proceeds. The result is often fascinating. At times the interviewer can sit back quietly and let the conversation flow. The possible shifts of meaning, however, make one wary of placing too much trust in any complex statistical analysis of comments. To do so would be like building a tower on sand. But where the discussion benefits from some straight-forward descriptive statistics—such as simple counts of how many statements are of one kind as against those of another type—we have added them.

Verbatim statements are not without their problems, of course. One that stands out for its vividness and naturalness may be lacking in precision. An example may be seen in the words of a sixth-grader in answer to the question: 'Why should people listen to your ideas?'. The question was taken to mean:'Why should politicians or people in government listen?'.

> If they were in Canberra ... I would listen to what other people's ideas are and what they think and get to know what everyone else in the world is ... And if I was a person in Canberra, I would listen ... because they are the people who make the decisions and other ... they might learn what other people don't like ... And other people get a fair chance to have their speak what they like better and what they would like to have.

Although the words have come tumbling out in a jumble, the concepts are fairly clear. If you don't listen, you may give people what you think they want rather than what they really want. People have a right to express what it is *they* like. And people in power have a special obligation to listen. Fortunately, most of the children's comments take less untangling.

We have avoided the identification or discussion of individual children but have given, with each comment quoted, the school-grade. On a few occasions we have contrasted directly the comments of younger children with those of older ones. Knowledge of a child's grade alerts us to differences between the ages and also to the fact that some types of perceptions and ways of working things out are present among quite young children.

We have also avoided making extensive references to the literature on child development. We have chosen instead to mention particular scholars in the text only where an idea is tied with some specificity to their work. The endnotes at the back of the book provide some useful reference material.

The book starts with two chapters related to the home setting. In one, the accent is on people: children's views on the togetherness of family life, on parents and on siblings. In the other, the accent is on activities: children's views on their jobs around the house and on what is involved in getting started on a school day.

The following two chapters are related to the school setting. Again, in one the accent is on people: children's views of teachers and their behaviour. In the other, the accent is on activities: children's views of what they do at school (both 'learning' and 'playing') and the changes they would like to see.

Chapter 5 deals with friendships, allotted a separate chapter because they often cut across the contexts of home and school, appearing in both even though they are especially prominent in the school setting.

The final chapter summarises the framework we have used, concentrating on the nature of settings. It also offers some directions for change based on the ideas brought to light by the children's comments.

Each chapter contains first several sections dealing with satisfactions and dissatisfactions: the good and not-so-good features of the aspect of life under discussion; the hopes, expectations, and real encounters. The chapter then moves to a consideration of how children make sense of each setting: the explanations they come up with, the rules they see as operating, the conditions they think should apply. The end of each chapter turns to the nature of individual differences and the ways in which they are handled.

First we look at the way children see family life, with an accent on people and relationships.

1
LIFE AT HOME:
people

In the setting of home and family life, children encounter a variety of people: parents, siblings and relatives. In this chapter, we explore children's comments on what 'family' means to them and what they observe, appreciate or hope for in family relationships. As the following few comments suggest, the picture is one with several facets to it, even when one considers only the immediate family:

> Good parents care for you. They spend money for you. They love you. They buy things for you, and they try to protect you when you're in desperate trouble. (Grade 5)

> They care for you and love you and spank you when you're naughty. (Grade 3)

> They care for you and take an interest in sport and that. (Grade 4)

> I wish my family would all sit down together for breakfast. (Grade 3)

> Mum and dad and my sister all love me. I don't know about my brothers. (Grade 4)

Our interest is in what children see as the main features of family relationships—the big issues—and how they work things out in the course of thinking about family life. We begin with a section on the general pleasures that children see in family life, and then take a closer look at what children appreciate in parents, and hope to see in their relationships with parents.

These sections are followed by one that concentrates on what children see as departures from the ideal: the imperfections of parents, the behaviour of one's siblings, the competing interests that threaten togetherness.

This combination of perfections and imperfections clearly calls for some mental effort if a child is to make sense of family relationships. We shall look at two areas where the children's comments show clear signs of mental work: their explanations for sibling friction and parents' behaviour.

The chapter ends with a section on individual differences, offsetting the focus on the majority that marks the earlier sections.

The pleasures of family life

The children's comments emphasise several pleasures and rewards in family life. One is a sense of 'being together'. Another is the sense of belonging to a larger group of people, especially true in a well-populated family with grandparents, aunts, uncles, cousins, babies and other relatives. A third is the sense of an unshakable bond. You belong to this group from the start and they 'will look after you all your life'. Another is the sense of being part of a world of sharing and mutual help: a world in which you both give and receive, need and are needed.

Children may not feel that family life always yields these pleasures. These are, however, the features they often speak about, hope to see, and treasure when they occur. We shall look at the most appreciated aspects of family life as the children describe them.

Being together

'What are the favourite things you like doing with your family?' 'Just sitting talking', 'talking over dinner', 'sitting by the fire', 'watching telly together' and 'just being with them' are frequently mentioned as the most favoured activities. 'I like it when all the family is together and we just talk over dinner and just have a few jokes together and just be together', explains a fifth-grader, managing to get three 'togethers' into one short sentence.

These family occasions are by no means restricted to the traditional nuclear family. Take for instance this fifth-grader's description of weekend barbecues in which a rather complicated family gets together:

I just like it when the family is having a good time and having a joke and a barbecue and they're nice and everyone's there ... they often are there ... and everyone drops in at lunch at one place and has lunch at the other and it's nice when you get together and have a joke and that. Then in answer to the question 'How many people in your family?' she replies:

Well, there is my stepfather and my mother; I've got two sisters, two stepsisters, one stepmother, and two halfbrothers. But there's only five of us live together now.

These special moments of togetherness need not be flamboyant occasions. 'We're a quiet family; we enjoy ourselves at home', says a sixth-grader. They can be at all times of the day, but are mentioned most often as occurring around meal times, or on outings. In talking about their holidays, for instance, one sixth-grader said, 'What I liked best was all sitting on the bed in the morning and working out what we should do', and another sixth-grader commented, 'It was fun when we were altogether in this one room and we stayed up late talking'.

Being together in these simple ways is seen by the children as having several advantages. One is that you simply have more fun:

Like if you go down to the river by yourself it's not much fun, but if you go with your family, you can do all sorts of things, or just talk. (Grade 5)

I like doing everything with the family because it's always better than one person. (Grade 6)

It's better doing things with your family because otherwise you might get bored sitting around doing nothing. When you go together you care more about each other. Like with two people even you get bored, but if you're with the whole family you never get bored. (Grade 4)

Another benefit is that being together allows you to do things or learn things that you normally would not. To choose some examples:

I like going on picnics with my family because you have more fun and you can go swimming and have games with your mother and father and sisters that you can't at home. (Grade 3)

I like going out in our boat with them because they teach you new things and if you're wondering what island is that and it's the first time you've seen it and you want to know—well the next time you go around it you say, 'Oh that's the island that my mum and dad told me about it'. (Grade 6)

Like if we go on bushwalks they might know a certain plant—what it is—and they might tell us about it. (Grade 4)

I like going out to the surf with my family. When we're on the surf rider, dad picks me up and he throws me into the waves and my mum is always waiting at the edge and she always stops me before I run into the brick part at the end. (Grade 6)

Finally, being together as a family is seen by children as a time when fewer squabbles occur among themselves. In the words of two sixth-graders:

If you don't get on with another member of your family, it makes it easier if you are all together.

When the family is together you have really good fun, and you don't have any fights with your brothers and sisters and they don't muck up.

Such comments are a first warning that the sense of togetherness is not constant. It may even be fragile and easily threatened. Later in this chapter we shall consider some of the factors that threaten togetherness.

From the comments we have just looked at, however, we can see that times of togetherness, often occurring around small events rather than grand occasions, are clearly moments with great meaning for children and a source of joy to many of them.

Belonging to a larger, continuing group

Contemporary discussions about the family often make a distinction between the extended family where parents and children live with other immediate relatives, the nuclear family consisting of one set of parents and their children, and the 'modified extended' family where parents and children do not live together with other relatives, but have a good deal of contact with them, and relatives help each other out when necessary. These discussions often make the point that the family isolated from relatives suffers from not having ready help available when needed. Our interview material highlights another important role played by relatives—providing the child with a sense of living in a well-peopled family, and a sense of being linked to both past and future. In answers to the question 'Is there someone you would like to spend more time with?', grandparents, aunts, uncles, cousins and still more distant relatives are often mentioned:

I wish that my grandmother and my grandfather and my aunties and uncles and my cousins and the whole family came with my friends so we can have a good time near the big house. (Grade 4)

I'd like to see all my grandparents and all my cousins in England because I left when I was six and I still haven't seen them till now but some of them might be coming next year. (Grade 6)

My big whole family so that we can talk to each other and have nice food and enjoy each other and play lots of games. (Grade 4)

What does a well-peopled family provide? Among several benefits, it provides novelty and change in a child's life, especially if you visit, but not only then:

I would like to spend more time with my auntie because I love it at her house and you have fun, and when she is at our house she is not so much fun. (Grade 6)

More time with my grandmother. When she comes, it lightens up the whole day. (Grade 5)

One's kin may also provide some forms of generosity and support that are special. Grandparents are mentioned especially often in this respect:

Nana gives me money to go up to the shops and buy things. (Grade 2)

My grandpa, he is a butcher and he gives me a sausage whenever I see him. (Grade 2)

My grandmother—well, she's dead now but when you had trouble she always said, 'Oh well, I'll help you out', and when she helped me out she'd always give me something, like 50 cents. (Grade 6)

Most of all, however, a well-peopled family provides children with a sense of lineage, of links to a continuing group. Adults talking about the past can at times be 'boring' to children, but we were surprised at how often a treasured form of 'sitting and talking' with the family was story-telling about some past experiences. These included anecdotes about a parent's childhood and any colourful episodes from their parents' or grandparents' lives. Such reminiscences seemed to help children gain a sense of who they were, and where they fitted into a larger picture. These children enjoyed:

Talking with my family about the olden days in Italy . . . the days of the war. (Grade 5)

> Sitting around talking about when mum and dad were kids.
> (Grade 6)
>
> Staying with grannie and my two sisters and just talking about
> things that have happened and that are going to happen. (Grade 5)
>
> Talking with them about when I was a baby. (Grade 5)

Some children were prepared to put up with quite a bit to get this feel for the past: like one fifth-grader who said she enjoyed 'going to parties with old-fashioned people being there' even though it was 'boring'.

Once again, it is grandparents who are singled out for special mention. To children, grandparents are concrete proof that one belongs to a continuing group. We had thought this function of grandparents might be less marked among the many children in Australia whose grandparents are in other countries. On the contrary, the feeling for grandparents seemed to be even stronger in this group. Grandparents are not only proof of belonging to a continuing group, but also proof of one's cultural heritage. 'The old country' may not be a strong reality for the children of immigrants, but grandparents are—even if you have never seen them. Consider, for instance, the following answers to the question 'Who would you like to spend more time with?':

> I'd like to spend more, well I haven't spent any time with this
> person because he is my grandfather and I never knew him, but if
> he was alive I would like to spend a whole lot of time with him.
> (Grade 5)
>
> I wish I was in the grave so I will be with granma and granpa.
> (Grade 4)
>
> My grandmother and my grandfather and my great great
> grandmother. (Grade 5)
>
> My granma in Italy. It would have meant everything to her to see
> me, only she died. (Grade 4)
>
> I would like to spend more time with all my family: not just my
> mother, father and brother but with my grandparents and all my
> family in Spain because I don't even know none of them. (Grade 4)

Members of a family may be distant, but the conviction remains for most children that these people do care about them and are still interested in them. 'It would have meant everything to her to see me' says it all.

An unshakable bond

Social scientists often distinguish between two routes to love or respect. In one, love or respect comes to you because of who you are: a father, a mother, a son, a daughter, or whatever. In the other, love or respect comes to you because it is earned. You have earned it by proving that you care or by offering something in exchange (for example, my loyalty in exchange for your financial support; my care of you now in exchange for your care of me later).

In any relationship, this line of thought continues, it is important to know what expectations people have about what comes as a right and what needs to be earned, especially since these different forms of feeling have different consequences. Earned love and respect, for instance, can bring a sense of competence, but if one is made to feel that they must be earned constantly ('What have you done for me lately?') these feelings can easily be lost.

What are children's expectations of family relationships? Some recognise that respect does, to a certain extent, have to be earned. A fourth-grader remarked, 'My dad thinks I'm important because I'm in the basketball team'. Others realised that earned respect needn't have primary importance; a fifth-grader stated, for example, 'They're proud of you when you win like, but they don't care if you don't'.

For the great majority of children, in fact, family love and care is a natural thing; it is freely given and they need not work for it or worry about losing it. As we shall see in the section on individual differences, there are children without this bedrock confidence in their family relationships. Most of them, however, hold the conviction that there is no question about parents looking after you, simply because of who you are and who they are:

When you go in the boat waterskiing, if you fall off, well you know they will come back after you. (Grade 4)

They love me because I'm theirs, you see. (Grade 3)

I'm all they've got. (Grade 2)

They care for me because I am the only one in the world like me. (Grade 3)

If I was killed, they would be upset for a lifetime. (Grade 5)

When I go out, they're lonely. (Grade 4)

Your future is everything to them. (Grade 5)

For some children, such as this sixth-grader, the biological aspect of belonging reinforces their conviction that they will be cared for: 'I think my mum and dad make a good parent because they. . .you were born to your mum and they should be the people to take care of you because you were born to them'.

The tie need not be biological, however. Caring is what parents do: for children born to them, for adopted children, or even for strangers.

> A parent cares for you and helps you and . . . like my little brother—he is adopted and when he was adopted mum bought him a baby set, as good a one as mine. (Grade 4)

> I like parents because if you're hurt or something they come out and look after you, even if it's parents who have never even met you. They sort of come out and look after you as if you were their own children. (Grade 5)

As these comments suggest, the sense of a freely given, unquestioned care is mentioned most often in connection with parents. They are the ones most often mentioned as 'caring for you all your life', as 'standing by you even when everyone else is against you', as 'there when you've got something personal to say and you don't want to say it to anyone else'. As we shall see in a later section, children see more in parents than just their caring attitude. But it certainly seems apparent that most children see one of the joys of family life as being the ability to rely on a bond that is different from that to be found with other people.

A world of sharing and mutual help

We have so far described three of the positive features children mention as being a part of family life: togetherness, being part of a continuing and well-peopled group, and being linked to others by an unshakable bond.

Another feature to be singled out is the sense of giving as well as receiving, of being needed: in other words, a sense of contributing something to family life and to the welfare of others. This is sometimes expressed very explicitly, and may even be felt by the youngest children:

> I go and pick mangoes—about 100 a day—and my father helps me, so I help him. (Grade 4)

I just be good for mum. Just sit down and read. I don't get in her way. (Grade 1)

In Chapter 2 we look more comprehensively at children's jobs around the house and the way these are seen to help parents. But household chores are not the only forms of contribution that children see themselves as making:

I'm carrying on the family. (Grade 6)

I wish I could spend more time with my aunty and cousin, because me uncle he's left them to us and I don't know, I just like to spend more time with my cousin because she feels a lot happier when Shane and I are with her. (Grade 3)

I go to see nan, beacuse pop is dead and she doesn't get much company. (Grade 3)

My cousin, he's eleven months old and I help bath him and feed him and that. (Grade 4)

The role of parents

We have outlined four of the aspects of family life that children appreciate and treasure. Obviously parents play a crucial part in most of these experiences. Parents generally create the occasions when family members can enjoy being together. They provide an introduction, an access route to a larger group. They provide the most unshakeable child bond and they are the most frequent focus of mutual help.

To gain a clearer picture of what parents can mean to children, we have looked particularly at the answers to three questions: 'Who is important to you?', 'Who are you important to?' and 'What makes a good parent?'.

The importance of 'mum' and 'dad'

When asked to write down an answer to the question 'Who is important to you?', 57 per cent of the children nominated 'mum', 'dad', or 'my parents'. Among other people mentioned, 'family' accounted for another 8 per cent, a friend for 12 per cent, God or Jesus for 12 per cent, and grandparents, relatives or siblings for a further 5 per cent. Parents predominated also in written answers to the question 'Who are you important to?': 'mum', 'dad' or 'my parents' accounted again for 57 per cent of all the people mentioned; family accounted again for 8 per cent, a friend for 10 per cent, God or Jesus for 8 per cent, grandparents, and siblings or relatives for a further 6 per cent.

These answers bring out not only the significance of parents, but also some differences between them. 'Mum' and 'dad' are not always seen in the same light. Forty per cent of children nominate both parents as being important to them and 42 per cent perceive that they are important to both their parents. Where a single parent is mentioned, however, it is mum who predominates. She receives 12 per cent of single-parent replies, compared with 4 per cent for fathers. The same pattern applies in terms of the people named as thinking the child is important to them: 42 per cent nominated 'mum and dad' or 'my parents', while mum received more single nominations (10 per cent) than did dad (5 per cent).

The generally stronger bond with mothers seems to apply to all ages. We had thought it might be especially true of the youngest children, but in fact it is reflected in every school grade's answers. If we take, for instance, the question 'Who is important to you?', the nominations for 'mum' alone and 'dad' alone are, respectively: 10 per cent against 6 per cent (Grade 1), 10 per cent against 6 per cent (Grade 2), 13 per cent against 5 per cent (Grade 3), 14 per cent against 1 per cent (Grade 4), 14 per cent against 5 per cent (Grade 5), and 15 per cent against 4 per cent (Grade 6).

Why the difference between mum and dad? To answer this question, we need to gain a clearer sense of children's perspectives on what parents do. Some of their perspectives begin to emerge in comments on their own mothers and fathers:

> I go to my mum; my dad never listens. (Grade 6)

> My father listens to me often. He respects me as the oldest, but my mother—she just takes me as one of the kids. If I'm in trouble, she says 'Sort out your own problems; if you can't do that, you can come back to me'. (Grade 6)

> My mum is most important to me because if she dies my dad would have to work overtime, and I would have no one to look after me. (Grade 6)

> Dad, because when we go places he pays for you. (Grade 4)

> She's always got something to cheer you up with. (Grade 5)

> Dad is more kind than me mum. (Grade 5)

> She knows all the problems. (Grade 4)

A more complete picture of children's perspectives emerges from their views on the qualities essential to being a good parent.

Definitions of a 'good parent'

In attempting to categorise children's answers to the question 'What makes a good parent?', we have grouped together the qualities mentioned which appear to be of a particular kind (for example, there were qualities mentioned which have to do with loving, caring and comforting, and others associated with teaching or taking a child to various places). The children usually mentioned more than one quality, and we have counted each one mentioned.

We have also divided the results according to age, treating Grades 1 and 2 as one group, Grades 3 and 4 as another, and Grades 5 and 6 as the oldest group. This highlights characteristics such as the apparent inclination of the youngest children to offer descriptions that are concrete and in physical terms ('They give you good food and take you places').[1] Older children are more inclined to give descriptions that are in terms of people's inner nature ('They have a sense of humour'; 'They want the best for you'). When we find a quality that is important for children of all ages, despite the differing 'languages' of description, we can feel sure that we are dealing with a continuing expectation concerning parents.

The results are shown in Table 1.1. To work through the table, using the children's words, we shall give some examples of the qualities which good parents are expected to have, noting which qualities are important at all age levels and at what stage others change in importance.

A caring attitude. The qualities most often mentioned as being essential for a good parent have to do with a variety of forms of caring. General statements about loving, caring, comforting (for example, 'They love you'; 'They care for you'; 'They're nice to you when you're in trouble') account for 27 per cent of all the qualities mentioned. They are also the most common at all age-levels (21 per cent, 31 per cent, 28 per cent).

Appreciated also are some specific ways in which caring may be expressed. One of these takes the form of providing material things. 'They feed you', 'give you toys', 'give you money', 'give you things', 'give you pocketmoney'. These specific forms of caring account for 6 per cent of all qualities mentioned, and are spoken

Table 1.1   The main qualities mentioned by children in their definitions of a good parent (shown as the percentage of all qualities mentioned)

	All grades	Grades 1 & 2	Grades 3 & 4	Grades 5 & 6
A caring attitude				
Loves, cares for, comforts you	27	21	31	28
Provides material things	6	15	5	3
Protects/looks after you	6	11	7	5
Does not hit/fight	4	3	2	5
Controls, but fairly	11	4	8	12
Total	54	54	53	53
Understanding and sharing				
Makes you feel special	8	19	9	3
Understands you	8	2	5	11
You understand them	2	3	2	2
Shares fun with you	3	3	4	3
Total	21	27	20	19
Helping to open up the world				
Gives access to people and places	9	10	11	8
Teaches, explains, shows	4	1	5	4
Total	13	11	16	12

Note: We have omitted all qualities that account for 2 per cent or less of those mentioned.

about most commonly in the early grades (15 per cent, as against 5 per cent and 3 per cent in the higher grades). It is not that the younger children are more mercenary. As mentioned previously, it is just that they tend to think and express themselves in more concrete terms at that age.

A further form of specific caring lies in the way good parents 'protect you and look after you'. Young children may at times appear to have no sense of danger. Their comments, however, bring out the extent to which they feel vulnerable and appreciate in parents the ability to protect them from a variety of threats:

They keep you from getting hurt. (Grade 2)

They stop you from being run over. (Grade 1)

When they go out they get a babysitter for you. It means they love you but if they just go out and leave you on your own it means they don't care. (Grade 3)

If you go out somewhere like riding on your bike, they say 'You be careful' and if you don't get back on time they will always go looking for you. (Grade 4)

I think when they just don't go and leave you alone on the street and walk off, they care for you a lot. (Grade 4)

If they tell you off for something and they don't let you go because it's only for your own safety, you might get hurt or something, I still like them. (Grade 4)

The hope of protection is one aspect of vulnerability. It lies in strong contrast to another aspect: the definition of good parents as those who are not themselves a source of danger and threat, who do not attack or hit their children. Three per cent of all qualities mentioned by children have to do with a good parent being someone who does not hit, belt, bash, kick, smack or—in one child's phrase—'throw you through a glass door'.

The fifth quality we have categorised as reflecting a caring attitude is the way in which good parents control their children in a fair manner. Parents are expected 'not to say yes all the time', 'not to give you everything you want', and 'not to let you do just anything'. Control, however, has to be exercised in a fair and reasonable fashion. This important quality accounts for 11 per cent of all those mentioned, and increases in frequency as children grow older. That increase may reflect the fact that discipline and control become more frequent as children grow older, or the fact that older children are more concerned with issues of justice and fairness and more inclined to wonder about how one can reconcile acts of loving care with acts of punishment.[2]

Understanding and sharing. Under this umbrella term, we have placed four qualities the children consider to be characteristic of a good parent: making you feel special, sharing fun with you, and the two sides of understanding—they understand you and you understand them. Within this group, we shall single out for comment only two points. One is that parents understanding you is mentioned more often than the reverse: you understanding them.

The other is that children in Grades 1 and 2 stand out for their frequent mentions of good parents as 'making you feel special' (19 per cent, compared with 9 per cent and 3 per cent in the older groups). Among these youngest children, the mention of being treated as special is often tied to their more physical descriptions: 'They cook the things *you* like', 'They buy the things *you* like'. The decline in this type of comment with increasing age is probably the result, again, of the fact that material perceptions of things become replaced, to a certain extent, by concepts such as 'fairness'. Good parents:

. . . listen to both sides. (Grade 4)

. . . give equal jobs to everyone in the family. (Grade 4)

. . . don't pick on one kid in particular. (Grade 5)

Helping to open up the world. Under this term, we have placed two important qualities. One is that parents teach and explain. They may, as we saw earlier, tell you the names of places and plants. They may explain their actions and yours, as expressed by a sixth-grader: 'If you do something wrong, your mother and father sits you down and tells you what you did wrong and explains why you shouldn't do it and what you can do'. They may also teach you some of the things teachers usually cover: 'Like my dad, he knows lots of sums and he does sheets for me and I work them out' (Grade 2).

The second important aspect of opening up the world is that through parents, you get to go places and meet people. Parents are your introduction to a world that might otherwise be unavailable to you.

The importance of this access is most easily grasped when we think of being taken to places and to the activities these allow. We were curious to see which activities were especially popular among those listed as 'favourite things to do with your family'. Perhaps because these were Australian children, the most commonly mentioned family outing was going to the beach in the daytime and—a special treat—at night, 'when there are little lights in the water and you get jellyfish'. One city child stated, democratically, that his favourite activities were going overseas and going to the beach. The next most favourite outings were (in order of popularity) bushwalks and picnics, camping and fishing trips, movies and restaurants, shopping for gifts, the zoo, the circus and Marineland. Overall, outdoor life was very much to the fore.

Through parents, also, children see themselves as coming to know other people. Parents are a child's entry point to a host of relatives and to a sense of being part of a larger and continuing group. In the words of a fifth-grader: 'Last year we went back to Italy and I met my grandparents and the whole village'.

Very clearly, the child with good parents in all the senses mentioned is indeed living in a secure and happy world. These children see the best of all possible worlds as one where all the good features of family life predominate, orchestrated by parents who are loving and caring, who open up a wider world of people and places, and with whom you have a special understanding and an easy exchange of ideas and feelings.

In the children's eyes, this is a perfect state. What do they see as the imperfections?

Threats to family happiness

Positive reports of family life are not the only side to children's perspectives. They do perceive threats to family bliss. We have singled out three that are often mentioned: the imperfect nature of parents, the competing interests of all members of the family, and sibling behaviour.

The imperfect nature of parents

The definitions of a good parent have already made it clear that all parents are not perfect. They do not always listen, share your interests, understand you, make wise settlements of disputes, or explain things, and they are not always both 'firm and gentle'. They can be 'bossy', 'not kind', 'busy', too readily inclined to 'scream at you', and—less often in these children's comments—at each other. They often seem inconsistent, saying yes sometimes and no at others. In the saddest cases, they may cease to care. Even the best may be puzzling. In the words of a fifth-grader: 'I think love is important, but sometimes they growl at you and then after they growl at you they say they growl because they love you. It just doesn't make sense'.

In the section on 'working things out', we shall be asking: How do children account for the imperfections or inconsistencies of parents? What advice do they give for such difficult areas as discipline? For the moment, to be fair to parents, we need to note that the qualities looked for in a good parent are sometimes in conflict with one another. Take the case of it being important to be both fair and also especially understanding. The wisdom of Solomon seems called for in the following case of double demand: 'I think a good parent is that they have to be understanding when, if your brother has just come out of hospital or something, and they keep raving on about it and they shout at you to do things' (Grade 5).

Competing interests

Parents are often described nowadays in the popular press as being too 'busy' to share activities with children. The special villain in the piece is thought to be the mother's involvement in paid work outside the home (the phenomenon of 'working mothers'). A good example of the expectations involved in such views may be seen in the comment of a third-grader who told the interviewer she would like to see more of her mother. 'Oh, your mother works, does she?', was the interviewer's spontaneous response. The child replied: 'No, I see a lot of her. It's just I like her a lot so I'd like to see *more* of her'.

We had expected to be discussing competing interests primarily in terms of the interests of parents. The children made it clear, however, that in their view the problem lies in the competing interests of *all* members of the family.

As they see it, their own involvement in school is one of the biggest problems for family togetherness. To take some examples:

I'd like to see more of my parents cause we're always at school. When you go home you go and have tea, watch a bit of T.V. and you go to sleep and then you wake up in the morning, have breakfast and go to school again. (Grade 6)

You can't really talk to them or help them much because you're at school doing your own work and it's boring. (Grade 4)

I just like to be with my whole family. [What stops you from being with them?] When I get home from school I have to do my homework and when I'm finished, my mother is cooking sometimes. My father comes home from work and he's tired and that, and my other sister also has to do homework and there's just my little brother and he likes to watch T.V. and play with little cars and everything. (Grade 6)

Siblings also are noted as developing interests that reduce family pleasures. Those especially commented on took the form of interests in other people. A sixth-grader, for example, after talking about the pleasures of family togetherness, was asked 'So you think families spend enough time with each other?'. She replied: 'No'. . . 'cause the most of the brothers go out to the girl-friend's place'. A younger child (a third-grader) has a sadder story: 'I'd like to see more of my sister cause she's married and I hardly ever see her 'cause my mother doesn't own a car and my brother is always out at work or out where my other brother lives . . . and her husband he never talks to you or anything and he never comes over and he never brings Cathy over'.

Are parents, then, exempt from being seen as having interests that compete with family life? Not at all. They too can display interests in other people that take away from their interest in you. The children remind us of their concerns about divorce, death, and remarriage, occasionally in first-person terms, but more often in animated discussions of people one has heard about. One particular example was the story of a widower 'in our street' who proposed marriage to a divorcee and was accepted on condition that 'he get rid of his own children because she didn't like them'. The general verdict was that such things happen and that such an attitude was a bad sign: 'He shouldn't marry her; she'd be cruel'.

Comments concerning the competing interests displayed by parents often refer to being somewhat ignored when others come to the house. A fifth-grader remarked, 'I admire parents when they mind and talk to you; when there are other adults there, they pay a bit more attention to you'.

Children can also feel a sense of regret that parents do not share their interests. To many children, happiness consists of shared interests:

I admire the attitude of some parents going out to play cricket with their children. (Grade 5)

I think it's love and a parent who sticks with you all the way in sporting fields and keeps you going. (Grade 5)

> If you had a mother and a father who liked everything same as you, it would be great. (Grade 3)

Most children recognise that parents do have other interests. A total sharing of interests is not possible. What would they like to see?

At this point, we need again to break 'parents' into mothers and fathers. The two are seen by the children as making quite different contributions to shared interests.

The difference is brought home first by answers to the question: 'Is there anyone you would like to spend more time with?'. Fathers were mentioned twice as often as mothers were. What gives fathers this special status? One reason is that *fathers are seen as less available to their children than are mothers*, as spending less time with children than the children would like. Far more often than for mothers, children comment on how 'busy' fathers are, even when at home:

> Dad's busy watching cricket. (Grade 4)

> I'd like to see more of my father. I don't get to see him much, because even when he's home, all the time he's rushing round. (Grade 4)

> Dad's got his own life to lead. (Grade 6)

> He's a scientist so we're not supposed to bother him. (Grade 2)

> I like one who is not running around all the time doing jobs and that. (Grade 6)

Mothers can be 'busy'—'sometimes she's cooking'—but fathers are the ones most likely to have all their time slots filled.

The other side to the special status of fathers is that *fathers are nonetheless more often mentioned as involved in fun activities*. When they do join in, it is often on outings and special events rather than in everyday routines. Fathers also stood out when children were asked: 'What do you like to do most with your family?'. When we counted up the specific references to people in these activities, fathers accounted for 46 per cent of the people mentioned, mothers for 21 per cent, brothers 15 per cent, sisters 16 per cent, other relatives 6 per cent, and pets 3 per cent.

There are some families where mum is the major fun-sharer because dad has opted out: 'We usually don't do things as a family but we do with mum. We play games at night because dad is usually lying down or reading or at work, and we go on picnics with mum' (Grade 4). In most cases, however, the father who joins in is seen as special, with regrets for a mother who does not 'play' or do novel things:

> My favourite is when dad cooks the Sunday roast and says 'Come on everyone' and we sit around the table and talk. (Grade 4)
>
> My father brings us somewhere outside and we play a lot, except my mother. (Grade 4)
>
> I like to play games but me mum won't play. (Grade 3)
>
> It's always me and dad that go out. Mum and me always stay home. I'd like to go out with me mum sometimes. (Grade 5)

Like fathers cooking Sunday roasts, mothers who play games ('My favourite is when mum gets on the trampoline') provide specially happy memories, perhaps because such role reversals reveal more of the real person inside the parent.

The comments are of particular interest because they fit with similar results from other groups of children, both in Australia and overseas.[3] Fathers, when involved, are more involved in play than are mothers. And they are more often seen by children as people you play with. Such results have prompted one Australian psychologist—Lorraine Riach—to ask parents: Fathers, when was the last time you took on some of the everyday routine of caring? Mothers, when was the last time you played or shared fun with your children?[4]

Sibling behaviour

The imperfect nature of parents, and the interests that compete with togetherness: these are the first two negative aspects of family life that children bring to our attention. The third is the behaviour of siblings. We quoted at the start of this chapter a fourth-grade child who carefully distinguished between members of the family: 'Mum and dad and my sister all love me. I don't know about my brothers'.

Sisters and brothers are not described in positive terms as often as are parents. At the same time, the picture is not completely black. To gain a balanced picture of children's views, we have counted up all the references to siblings in the discussions of family and asked how many are positive, how many negative.

Within the total group of children, 51 per cent of the comments are positive and 49 per cent are negative. There is not a great deal of difference in opinion between the various age groups, but what difference there is takes the form of an increasingly critical attitude. Among children in the first three grades, for instance, positive comments occur in 66 per cent of cases. Among the latter three grades, the figure drops to 51 per cent.

The positive remarks about siblings cover a range of helpful acts. Older brothers and sisters can play with you, teach you things, protect you, make your whole life more enjoyable: a fifth-grader said simply, 'They make me laugh'. Younger brothers and sisters offer you the chance of being the helper or the teacher: 'I'd like to spend more time with my brother, the handicapped one, because I'd like to teach him to do more things. At the moment I'm teaching him to play soccer pretty good' (Grade 5).

What do siblings do to attract negative remarks? For a start, they are often 'bossy'. They try to tell you what to do, as if they were parents. Moreover, they often back up their positions with physical force. Take some comments make in answer to a question, 'Does anything stop you from doing what you like to do?':

> My brother is what's wrong with our family. He's too big for his boots. (Grade 3)

> My big sister: because she is bigger, she hits me and torments me, and she's really cruel. (Grade 3)

> He bashes me up all the time because he's bigger than me. (Grade 3)

> We got this new television game and it's just one for the family and I say, 'Can I play for once', and the girls say 'No' and they belt you over the room and they get it and play it themselves, 'cause I've got three sisters and I'm the only boy and mum is always on their side. (Grade 4)

> Neil, my brother. He tricks me. He says 'Give me your bag'. And he might say he'll give you 50 cents and then he doesn't. (Grade 3)

To make things worse, siblings have a way of interfering with your relationship to your parents. They 'get you into trouble':

> It's not fair because I'm the eldest and Michael my brother he just ... say he came in and he pulls my hair or something or I say

'Don't do that' and my brother goes in and he says 'Mummy, Diane hit me'. (Grade 6)

My little brother: he takes things from me to get me into trouble because then I start punching him and I get blamed for punching first. (Grade 4)

My sister always says I started it, then mum belts me, but I don't. (Grade 4)

Siblings may also compete to be the one their parents like best, the one 'most important' to them. 'The boys are [more important] because dad can't stand taking out the girls because they're too noisy, but he takes me and me brother fishing and that' (Grade 4).

Finally, siblings can interfere with your freedom of movement and your relationships with friends:

My little sister ... If I'm invited to a birthday party, my little sister wants to come and she has to come but I have to ask the people who invited me can she come; but if she's invited to a birthday party I'm not allowed to go. If I go upstairs to my bedroom she goes upstairs to her bedroom, if I go to the toilet she waits outside for me, if I go into the kitchen she goes into the kitchen ... she's three. (Grade 5)

I wish I didn't walk my little brother to school and could go with my friends. (Grade 4)

They say I steal their friends, just because I play with them. (Grade 4)

In short, there are many ways in which the children see siblings as a problem. We shall look more closely at the positive aspects of sibling relationships in the section on individual differences.

Working things out: why do people behave as they do?

Psychologists spend much of their working time in trying to explain behaviour, with special attention given to the understanding of motives. In recent years, increasing recognition has been given to 'implicit' or 'informal' psychology, to 'conventional wisdom', and to everyday theories of motivation and development.[5] As these everyday explanations come under study, it has become clear that people put a great deal of effort into coming up with explanations and justifications. It has also become clear that one person's explanation can differ markedly from another's, and that we often choose the explanation that presents our own cause in its best light.

Where do children stand? We shall consider their explanations for the behaviour of siblings and parents.

Children's accounts of sibling friction

Most of the explanations offered by the children are what psychologists call 'single-factor explanations'. The problems stem from what the other person does or—less often—from what I do, but not from both of us.

In the case of sibling friction, the difficulties are almost always placed at the siblings' door. 'She's cruel'; 'they're rotten'; 'they're spoilt'; 'he's too big for his boots'.

Do the children really believe these simple explanations or are they just a way of arguing a case to themselves and to their parents? Two points incline us towards the view that children do in fact know better.

One is that their comments are less one-sided when they are talking about families other than their own. A particular example comes from one senior discussion group. After a litany of complaints about siblings, the interviewer was led to describe her own problem with her two sons who kept running to her accusing each other of having 'started it'. What should she do, she asked. How should she go about finding out which one was in the right? The answer was firm. 'They should both be punished the same for both fighting and causing the trouble'. In effect, other people's behaviour can attract more even-handed or sophisticated explanations than one's own, a result in line with studies of attribution in other contexts.

The second source of doubt about real views comes from a small group of children who are open in their admission that fighting with one's siblings can be fun:

I like bashing up me little brother [Why do you do that?] because it's fun. (Grade 4)

I like stirring me sisters, getting them into trouble, like when dad says there's too much girls in the house and stuff like that and I like belting into them ... And I like having fights with me mum. (Grade 4)

The notion that 'stirring me sisters' or brothers can be fun is not one that children are always open about or that parents always like to recognise. The children's comments, however, are a reminder to us that 'stirring', teasing, and fighting can be enjoyable and that the explanations for children not being able to get along with one another need not always be sought in the deep recesses of their souls or in the way parents have brought them up.

Children's accounts of relationships with parents

In looking at explanations for sibling friction, we considered some ways in which explanations in general may differ from one another: in the extent to which they are single-factor or multi-factor, and in the extent to which they present the self in the best possible light. The comments on parents bring out a third aspect of explanations: the extent to which they appear to be handed down by others or worked out for oneself.

Two areas serve as illustrations. These are the way parents respond to children's requests, and the way they combine discipline with love and fairness.

Requests and responses. Children make many requests of parents: requests to have things bought, to be given help, to be allowed to go places or do things not normally allowed. In responding to these requests, parents may sometimes say 'yes' and sometimes 'no'. What sense do children make of parents' answers? And what reasons do they offer to explain why parents should answer in a particular way?

We shall concentrate on comments about parents saying no. The first point to emerge is that children expect parents to say no some of the time:

A good parent is being understanding and strict, and not always saying yes all the time. (Grade 4)

They shouldn't spoil them so when they grow up they think they can get everything. (Grade 5)

I think parents should be strict in some ways, but not too strict. But they are not to spoil you, like when you say 'I like that' and they buy it for you and they give you some things sometimes when you ask for them, but say no the rest of the time. (Grade 6)

A good parent cares for you and they sometimes let you do something and sometimes they don't. (Grade 5)

> They shouldn't do it all for you. The children need to learn now or later on they won't even try. (Grade 5)

> If it's good for you, they should give it to you. But if it's not good for you, then they would be wrong to let you have it. (Grade 6)

To our ears, these explanations for saying no have a fairly adult sound to them. There is, in fact, an adult ring to three lines of argument that emerge in many children's accounts of why parents say no: parents act for the child's own good; parents know better; children often have a short-term view (that is, they do not always act in their own best interests). These forms of explanation appear in the comments just quoted and in some other examples:

> Well, say there's this old house and it looks real interesting but they say 'Don't go in' and you do, and it's all rotten and you could break your leg and lie there for days . . . well, you should *listen*. (Grade 6)

> Some people say, 'No, I don't want to go to school' and the big people decide. They have to make the decision not the children. If you left a bowl of lollies and a bowl of food you would eat the lollies more than the food, but they know what is best for you. (Grade 5)

What do the children themselves add to these arguments, or do they stop at a simple acceptance and repetition of parents' perspectives? One addition is that the restrictions should come with an explanation: 'I like a parent to be kind to you and give you something if you want it, and if it is not worth it, well, they just explain why you can't have it' (Grade 6). Another is that the restrictions should be thoughtful and should fit the case. Comments along these lines were especially clear in discussions of whether and when parents should help children or encourage them to work things out for themselves:

> If you have something hard and you can't work it out, they sit up and talk to you about it. Then you would be much better off, because if they don't tell you what to do you just have to work it out for yourself. And say if you tried to fix the frypan for your mother and if you have to teach yourself, well then you are in hospital for a couple of days and then it is really bad. (Grade 5)

The third addition concerns questions about whether parents do always know best. 'They don't always know', says a fifth-grader. And at times their information is too anchored in the past:

I like a parent that listens to both sides, and because you are the youngest you don't sort of get into trouble because of something you should have done that your sister did when she was your age. (Grade 6)

Well, a good parent is one that gives you some discipline and stuff like that and telling you not to do things, and letting you do some things that you're an expert at, like climbing the tree in the backyard. When I was about four or five years old, when a boy named Justin came along, he was six years old and he taught me how to climb trees 'cause he knows how to climb every tree in the world .. well my mum, she didn't know. (Grade 3)

Part of the task of growing up and of working things out, it appears, consists of figuring out the areas where parents 'know best' as against those 'that you're an expert at'.

Combining discipline with love and fairness. This is the second area where we observe children expending a great deal of effort in searching for an explanation, and mixing together ideas that are handed down with some ideas of their own.

We need to face the fact that it is not easy for children (or for anyone) to form a coherent image from the fact that a person who loves and understands you may also punish you, with the punishment often being painful. Some parents avoid the dilemma, keeping for themselves the nurturing role and assigning the disciplinary role to someone else (teachers, or the other parent). 'Wait till your father comes home' is the classic example. Most of the time, however, the one person plays all parts.

What do children make of such a mixture of behaviour? A few admit frankly that it puzzles them. To repeat an earlier quotation: 'Sometimes they growl at you and then after they growl at you, they say they growl because they love you. It just doesn't make sense'. For every one of these children, however, we found three or four who stated firmly that it was a parent's job 'to teach you right from wrong' and that disciplinary actions are carried out mainly because a child is 'naughty' and are for the child's own good:

A good parent ... brings you up and is friendly to you and they hit you when you're naughty. (Grade 5)

They're good when they spank you when you're naughty. It helps you when you grow up not to be like bad people. Their mothers and fathers probably didn't spank them. (Grade 3)

A bad parent is when you get spoilt and [if] you do something bad, they just let you go and you would probably become a juvenile delinquent. (Grade 5)

If we didn't get told off, we'd probably be like those guys that go around who haven't learned anything. They kill people and that. (Grade 4)

If you don't get punished, that means your parents ... they don't care too much what happens to you, and if they punish you that means they are a good parent. (Grade 6)

If you break a glass and you blamed it on your sister and you don't own up and your mum and dad find out you done it, and if they let you get away with it they aren't sort of good parents. But if they don't, they're good parents. (Grade 5)

Only an occasional voice questions the wisdom of following parents' advice: 'It's good when they tell you not to do things like go with a stranger, although probably you would still go' (Grade 4).

In most of the comments we have just looked at, it is easy to hear the voices of parents. It is also easy to see that children need to believe that parents' actions are always for the child's benefit. To believe otherwise is to expose oneself to the thought of simply not being cared for. Where then do we begin to see signs of children working things out for themselves?

The signs of independent thinking tend to centre around the way in which disciplinary action should be taken:

They shouldn't hit you when you didn't do nothing. (Grade 4)

A good parent would smack you right away; a bad parent puts them in corners and says you're going to get a belt. (Grade 4)

A good parent is when they get angry; they say 'Right, that's it', and they give you a punishment, and it is all forgotten about. (Grade 5)

I think there should be love and affection, and they should be responsible for what the kid has done. Say if you were caught smoking, talk to him and have a discussion instead of like throwing him through a glass door or something. (Grade 5)

Like if they kick the kids if they do something wrong, well that's not a very good parent but if they just yell at you for doing something wrong, it's pretty good. (Grade 6)

A good parent doesn't hit kids, because they were kids once and they know what it's like to be hit when you don't do nothing. (Grade 6)

Just screaming at you, that's enough. (Grade 4)

In short, most of the children put their mental effort, not into challenging the right of parents to take disciplinary action or to mete out justice, but into working out some guidelines as to how this might best be done. We shall see this explanatory work come into full force when we look at comments on the disciplinary actions of teachers in Chapter 3. When children discuss teachers, they begin to sound like constitutional lawyers: far more so than they do with parents. Even in discussing parents, however, a great deal of time and effort is clearly put into understanding whether or not a certain disciplinary action is truly reasonable. It is, then, an unusual child in primary school who questions not the conditions of physical discipline but the legality and right of parents to use it at all:

> Well when they don't slap you when it's not my fault, my brother does it double and if they smack me I scream at them 'cause it wasn't my fault. Then next time I dob on him. I hate my mum and dad screaming at me and I wish they wouldn't smack me as much and I wish I lived in—forget what it is called . . . Switzerland, something like that. [Why?] It's a place where you are not allowed to smack kids. (Grade 3)

Individual differences

We have been presenting so far a general picture of two aspects to family life: its mixture of pleasures and problems, and the necessity for particular ways of working things out. Up to now, we have concentrated on the general picture, the majority view. Not all children, however, fit this general picture. We need to take note of individual differences. As we noted in the Introduction, that means we need to find some ways of describing variations between families: variations that avoid superficial categories such as rural and urban, lower income and middle-income, advantaged and disadvantaged.

From the comments on family life, we have drawn out two areas of variation between children. One area has to do with the way children work things out. The other has to do with the balance of positive and negative aspects in a child's family life. Since ways of working things out have been the subject of the preceding section, and will thus probably still be fresh in the reader's mind, we will look first at this source of idividual differences.

Ways of working things out

Children differ first of all in *the extent to which they need to explain things to themselves and others.* If you are punished painfully and often, and you still need to believe that you are loved and cared for, you will clearly need to work harder at building a coherent and acceptable account than if you are treated firmly but gently. The literature on abused children and abused spouses is full of desperate efforts to explain harsh behaviour ('only when he's tired or drunk'; 'only when she's had a hard day'; 'only when I deserved it').

Most of children's comments deal with less dramatic experiences. Nonetheless, some are clearly faced with more need for explanatory work than others. For some, the need stems from a difference between the way their family operates and the way other families function. Children in immigrant families are often in this position. Witness this example of a family pattern justified by a special concern for the child's benefit and the awful future likely to be ahead if the family pattern is not followed:

> I think a good parent doesn't let you go out as much as the Australian people do. My parents don't because they like me to grow up as one of the women in their country, instead of this country. Because this country is a good country, but there are too many people who go on drugs and out in the street. The parents should care for them and not just let them go like that. (Grade 6)

In some other cases, the notion that your needs count a great deal is simply difficult to reconcile with parents' actions:

> CHILD: I do think children should have pets 'cause they're fun to play with and you learn to look after them and when you grow up you know about animals.
> INTERVIEWER: Have you got a pet?
> CHILD: No. I did have but they took it to the pound.
> INTERVIEWER: Why ?
> CHILD: 'Cause he was annoying mum because he always was jumping in the car everytime mum pulled in the driveway.

Children differ also in *the kinds of explanations likely to be*

made available. One form of variation has to do with the availability of 'important' explanations. By and large, we all tend to offer
explanations—when turning one thing down for another, for
example—that stress the importance of the alternative we choose.
Families differ, however, in the ease with which they can offer
explanations for, say, parents being busy. Here are some that
sound highly acceptable:

> He's a scientist, so we can't bother him.
> She's a doctor, and she needs to help a lot of people.
> He's in the army, and has to be away a lot on courses.

Such simple, obvious explanations are not as readily available
to parents who wish only to point out that they need time to
themselves, or would really prefer watching sports on television to
actually playing the same sports with their children. 'Dad's busy
watching cricket' has a less sturdy ring to it than 'Dad's a
scientist', and may be less easy for children to accept.

Families differ also in the extent to which the explanations they
offer take the form of an emphasis on the dangers of the outside
world. We have already noted references to 'people on the street
taking drugs', and the possibility of readily becoming a 'juvenile
delinquent'. Some references to pets again draw a picture of
abounding dangers:

> I don't think children should have pets because if they run out on
> the street one day they could get dirty, and when you come and
> play with them and you don't know where they've been and they
> might have a disease and then you get sick and you might die.
> (Grade 6)
> You should have a dog. When you grow up and get to the age of
> being a young woman, you can have a watchdog on a leash for
> someone who might go and rape you. You can get the dog off the
> leash and he'll go after them. (Grade 5)

Finally, children differ in the *extent to which they present adult
explanations*. The majority of children appear to accept without a
quibble many adult explanations of family patterns, although one
must allow for some bias towards adult-type explanations when
the interviewer is an adult. Here and there, however, are some
voices that stand out as taking a clearly non-adult view. An

example is a child who happily states that he enjoys being aggressive towards his mother (either in reality or in fantasy):

> I like going to the beach 'cause . . . we get the shovel and we dig these huge big holes by about 3 feet big and then you cover them over with bracken and everything and then you scoop the sand over the top and when you get cranky with mum you build one and then you call her over and she walks straight across the trap and goes down—it's so good! (Grade 5)

The balance of pleasures and problems in family life

Families naturally vary in the extent to which either the positive or negative experiences dominate in their life together. We will look at two such variations: first, the degree of sibling rivalry and friction in families, and second, the extent to which children can turn to people who care.

The extent of sibling friction. We have noted earlier that half of the references to siblings are positive, and half negative. What might account for such differences?

For help with this question, we shall need to turn to some psychological theory, rather than rely only on the children's comments.

One line of theory would suggest that sibling rivalry largely concerns the present, combined with some past learning.[6] This point of view lays stress on the fact that friction between siblings is a fairly safe way to let off steam or be aggressive, 'to walk your wits' as one child put it. Fighting with siblings has fewer consequences than fighting with other people. No-one is likely to be seriously hurt, if only because parents are likely to act as umpires and can be called in by the loser. And the relationship cannot be easily broken. You may lose a friend if you try being bossy, but siblings are usually there the next day for a truce or a new round. In short, they offer opportunities for practice in both testing the limits of one's power and repairing the relationship at a later time.

In support of this view of everyday sibling friction would be the comments we have noted earlier on 'stirring' as 'fun'. If we followed it through, we might conclude that one source of difference between families is the extent to which children have learned that this form of aggression is relatively safe, enjoyable, and sometimes tacitly approved or accepted as inevitable.

A different line of theory—put forward by Freud—is intriguing, but is less easy to support from the children's comments, since the reasons are thought to lie in the unconscious. Freud considered that each human infant yearns for, and believes it has the right to, its mother's total supply of love and affection. This claim is most reluctantly abandoned as the growing child gradually becomes aware of the competing claims of other family members. More precisely, the claim is abandoned but the underlying sense of right remains. The child solves this psychologically stressful situation by concluding that if it can't have more than anyone else, then at least it shall have no less. It becomes a most zealous policeman over the activities of siblings. But there is more to it than that, in Freud's view. Beneath the skin of the policeman is the disenfranchised heir, now turned thief, ever ready to steal a march on the rivals. Within each family household each youthful policeman-thief works out his or her own strategies and alliances, depending on the number of siblings, their ages, sex, temperaments and other factors.

If we took a Freudian view, how would we account for differences in sibling rivalry and friction? One factor would be the age at which the child needs to work out the problem of being displaced. Freud, for instance, saw attitudes of rivalry as carrying over into the world at large, but considered that these newer relationships, undertaken as they are at a later and more rational age, generally lack the passion and intensity of sibling bonds. Thus 'fair exchange' between more mature mates and friends is acted out according to reasonably rational and agreed-upon rules. The same greater rationality might also be more possible for an older than for a younger child at the time when a new baby appears on the scene.

For some further suggestions, one might well turn to recent work by Dunn and Kendrick in England. 'Dunn and Kendrick were interested in a group younger than the children we have been considering but their findings have implications for older children as well. They followed up a group of families from the birth of the second child. The best relationships developed (and were maintained) where both children were the same sex; the older child's temperament was cheerful and not too intense; his or her relationship with the mother before the birth was not *too* idyllic; and where the mother was successful in enlisting the child as co-expert in caring for the baby and in depicting the baby as someone with a particular interest in the child (for example, 'he wants to see what you're doing'). Dunn and Kendrick's observations make it clear that it is worthwhile preparing the older sibling for the arrival of the new child. First reactions are important, because they have a high likelihood of persisting. Their observations also make clear just what problems an older child can face. Conversations between mother and child changed drastically after the birth, with the baby supplanting the child as the major topic of interest. The babies also consistently got their older siblings into trouble, by exciting them into activities that the parent then had to prohibit. These seem to be problems that may well vary from family to family, accounting for differences in the amount of sibling friction.

The presence of people who care. This is the second area we wish to consider as an example of individual differences in the balance of pleasures and problems in family life.

For a start, not all children feel cared for. For example, 3 per cent of children in this sample said 'no-one' when asked, 'Who are you important to?'. Neither do all children see parents as people they want to spend more time with:

> I don't like parents. (Grade 4)
>
> There's nothing much I really like doing with my family. I don't like being with them. I prefer to go with my friends. (Grade 6)

Even amongst those who do not hold negative views of parents, there are differences in the extent to which a child has other resources to rely on: others who can serve as extra 'safety nets' in times of trouble. Grandparents, as we have seen, can play this role. In Australia especially, they are likely to be more available to some children than to others. In one school, for instance, the discussion group of ten children contained two for whom all grandparents were in Greece, two with grandparents in Italy, one with grandparents in Turkey and one with grandparents in Portugal.

Some children can call on people other than relatives to create a sense of a well-populated support system. An example is a sixth-grader:

> I'd like more time with my uncle. Well, he's not my real uncle but

he's related to my father. He's father's blood brother and he's
Japanese and he's coming here for Christmas.

For other children, pets can play a safety-net role:

I think children should have pets because if your mum and dad yell
at you and tell you to go up to your room and you think that you're
going to run away or something, well you've got someone to talk to.
(Grade 6)

What happens when parents fail you and the usual safety nets
are absent? Two sisters provide an example. One was in fifth
grade, one in third, and by chance one was included in the junior
and one in the senior discussion group. The sisters were living in
foster care in a town several hundred miles away from the city
where the rest of the family lived. Asked about her favorite activity
with the family, the older child replied:

Just seeing them . . . because I haven't seen half of my family for
three or four years. Sometimes they come down and visit. I saw my
mother in June. [How do you feel about not seeing them for so
long?] You sort of forget them and you sort of say, I'm going to
bash myself up and that, you know. You forget about them.

The younger sister was asked what she thought was special
about her family.

CHILD: I don't know.
INTERVIEWER: What do you like doing with Mr and Mrs R.
[foster parents]?
CHILD: I like working for them.
INTERVIEWER: What's special about them?
CHILD: They take good care of me.
INTERVIEWER: You like them a lot?
CHILD: Yes.
INTERVIEWER: What's special about them?
CHILD: They take a lot of care of you.

The two sisters have reacted in different ways to the absence of
parental care. Kate who is older, seems angry, but also wishes to
forget about the family. The younger sister appears submissively
grateful for being taken care of at all. Both types of reaction stand
as a dramatic contrast to the cheerful confidence of the majority of

children that parents are powerful, resourceful, and inclined by nature—for all their imperfections—to provide love, understanding and care.

2

LIFE AT HOME:
activities

To understand any setting, we need to know about both the people involved and what they are doing: the cast of characters and the action. In the previous chapter, we have concentrated on the cast of characters and on children's views and feelings about people in the home setting. In this chapter, we turn to activities: more specifically, jobs around the house, and getting started in the morning.

What are the special features of these activities? The inter-weaving of people and activities is one feature. Most house jobs are done for other people: they are generally undertaken at the request or the command of others. Most of the morning's activities call for combining what you yourself do with what others are doing. In that rush to be ready, people can help get things done or can make life difficult in many ways, such as waking you up before you are ready, staying too long in the bathroom, or 'starting fights when you are in a hurry'.

A second major feature is the way activities are linked with one another. To alter one often means a change in others. If you sleep in, for instance, something else will usually need to be altered.

A third feature is that many activities are linked to the clock. They have to be done either at a certain time, or within a certain time.

These three features give rise to a sense of considerable pressure in some children, making them sound more like harassed executives than the carefree creatures one might take them to be:

I wish school didn't start until about a quarter to eleven so that we can make our beds, tidy our room, have a shower, clean our teeth and have a good breakfast. Then you might have time to watch a little television and you don't have to rush. (Grade 5)

You have to wake up early in the morning and you have to get dressed and come to school and then, after all that hard work, they give you more hard work. (Grade 3)

These features give rise also to two themes that will be prominent in this chapter: *children's feelings about time and about choice*. These are feelings we shall need to understand if we are to begin thinking about ways of improving children's worlds.

In looking first at jobs around the house, and then the activities involved in getting started on a school day, we will be considering what the children see as the main issues as well as the way they work things out, looking both at the general picture and individual differences as in the previous chapter.

The children were asked several questions about activities at home. Two of these were specifically about jobs around the house. The first was: 'Do you have any special jobs around the house?'. The second question was: 'Why do you do jobs around the house?'. Several further questions dealt with the start of the day: 'What time do you get up?'; 'How long does it take you to get to school?'; 'What did you eat for breakfast?'. At the end of these questions came one that yielded especially illuminating answers: 'If you could change one thing in the morning, what would it be?'. To this question each child wrote out an answer. We present these as they were written, adding a change of spelling in brackets only when it seems necessary for the meaning.

Since the question about changing the morning's activities includes the two areas of discussion (jobs around the house and getting started in the morning) we shall look at answers to this question first.

The first striking feature is that of the 2000-odd children, only 22 came up with no suggestions ('I don't know') or proposed keeping the status quo (for example, 'I wish for no change please because I like it now'). The next striking feature is the extent to which wishes deal with issues of time (e.g. 'wish I had more time in the morning') and with issues of choice ('wish I could', 'wish I didn't have to'). Time and choice account for 67 per cent of the juniors' wishes and 90 per cent of the seniors' wishes for change in the morning. The difference between juniors and seniors comes from the fact that the juniors often forgot or misunderstood the interviewer's instructions and expressed a wish close to the heart, but unrelated to the morning: for example, 'I wish to go to Disneyland' or 'to have a new bike'. Almost one quarter of the wishes expressed by the juniors' were of this kind.

Figure 2.1 takes all the wishes that have to do with time, with choice or with a mixture of both, and shows how often each of these occurs. It shows that both juniors

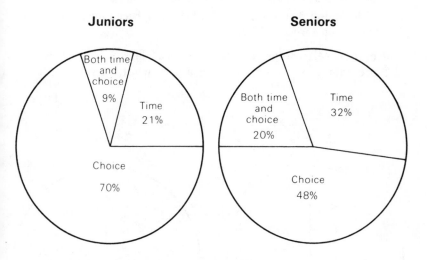

Juniors

Both time and choice 9%

Time 21%

Choice 70%

Seniors

Both time and choice 20%

Time 32%

Choice 48%

Figure 2.1   Children's wishes for a change in the morning
The distribution of wishes about time ('wish school was in the afternoon'), about choice ('wish I didn't have to walk to school', 'wish I didn't have to feed the ducks'), and about both time and choice ('I would like to stay in bed longer, but I can't, I have to go to school'; 'I wish they set the jobs, but we could decide when to do them).

and seniors are strongly concerned with issues of time and choice, (choice especially). The seniors more often mention both issues:

> Wish I did not have to get up and that school was in the afternoon. (Grade 4)

Wish someone would make my breakfast and I could get to school earlier. (Grade 4)

Wish I could do my jobs after school. (Grade 4)

It is also mainly the seniors who make it clear that time and choice are closely interrelated:

I wish school started at 10 a.m. because I could sleep in. (Grade 5)

I would like to stay in bed longer, but I can't, I have to go to school. (Grade 6)

Wish I could get up at 9.00 a.m. and still be erly [*sic*] for school (in other words school start in at 10.00 a.m.) (Grade 6)

I wish I didn't do the vackume [*sic*] cleaning because I would get to the bus stop earlier. (Grade 4)

Are there other ways of dividing wishes? There are, and Figure 2.2 presents one of them. It gives a somewhat finer breakdown

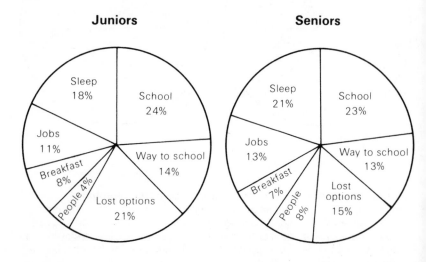

Figure 2.2   Children's wishes about the morning, in answer to the question: 'If you could change one thing in the morning, what would you change?'
These wishes account for 91 per cent of juniors, and 92 per cent of seniors' wishes. The remainder are in a 'miscellaneous' category.

and tells us what particular aspects of the morning children see as in need of improvement. For both juniors and seniors, the big issues are sleep (almost always the wish for more), school (mostly in the form of it starting later), the way to school (mostly in the form of a faster or more varied form), and alternatives to school—all the lovely things you might do if you didn't have to go to school, make your bed, fix your lunch, feed the cat etc. The general lack of difference between juniors and seniors is again striking. Once we begin school with its fixed start, apparently, the morning round puts the same harness on us all, and gives rise to much the same view of activities and their requirements.

Jobs around the house

The actual jobs are of less interest to us than are children's views and feelings about them. Two features of the actual jobs, however, are worth noting. The first is that almost all children have jobs to do around the house. Only 4 per cent report 'no special jobs' and these were all juniors. The second is that the jobs are a mixture of self-care (such as making one's own bed, cleaning one's room, putting one's clothes or toys away) and of help that benefits the whole family (for example, chopping wood for the fire, setting the table, vacuuming). They are also a mixture of 'inside' and 'outside' jobs, as indicated by reports from three busy fifth-graders:

'Feed the cat, vacuum, weed the garden'.

'Feed the birds, feed the dogs, and sometimes help mum put out the washing. Clean down the horses, help put up new fences for the stables, help mum do the dishes, clean our beds and make them again do the vacuuming and sometimes I have to clean out the bathroom and the shower'.

'Fill the woodbox, empty the rubbish, vacuum the floor'.

The positive side of household jobs

Children, as parents know, usually have mixed feelings about their tasks around the house. We shall start with what they see as the good features. The first two involve the reasons for doing the jobs; the third is concerned with the possibilities for togetherness. *They are your contribution.* Of all the reasons given by children for doing jobs—either spontaneously or in answer to the inter-viewer's question—more than half are concerned with helping others (58 per cent of juniors' reasons, 62 per cent of seniors'). Even the youngest have a sense of being helpful. In the words of some first-graders:

> 'I just be good for mum. Just sit down and read. I don't get in her way'.
> 'I try not to fight with my sisters'.
> 'I play outside and keep out of mum and dad's way'.

The help is for someone who needs it. Children often stop at saying that they do jobs simply 'to help', without specifying who is being helped. Where people are mentioned, they are almost always parents, and the parent most often named is 'mum' (72 per cent of the juniors' mentions of a parent, 61 per cent of the seniors'). She is seen as needing help for many reasons. 'She has a heavy load and a lot of other things to do' is the most common type of reason. She may also 'be expecting', 'have a bad back' or 'aches in her legs', be 'not young any more', 'tired', or 'in a hurry'. Her requests for help are usually reported as legitimate.

The tasks are often companionable. A number of jobs are done with someone you enjoy working with or being with. These remarks about company carry a strong reminder of divisions by gender: jobs done with dad being 'outside' and with mum 'inside'. The children help dad build a brick wall, mow the lawn, wash the car or pick fruit. By contrast all but 5 per cent of the references to helping mum involve 'inside' jobs: washing up, cleaning the house, looking after children, helping with the laundry. The rare references to mum emerging from the house are mainly to do with gardening, 'helping with the cows' and 'washing mum's car'. One's heart warms to the third-grader who commented, 'I help mum: I go jogging with her'. This is one of the rare mums who (as the children report it) engages in any form of leisure activity.

The real picture is almost certainly not as black-and-white as that may seem. For one thing, primary-school children are well known for the black-and-white quality of their descriptions of what males and females do: they regularly escalate probabilities into a world with no exceptions. Even those whose mothers are doctors or school principals may assert that women cannot be doctors or school principals[1]. Nonetheless, the association of mum with 'inside' routine jobs and dad with 'outside' jobs that seem more interesting is a reminder of the difference noted in the preceding chapter that fathers are linked more often than mothers to 'fun' activities.

The negative side of household jobs

The work is not always seen as helping someone else. Although the most frequently given reason is 'to help', some see it more as a transaction, or even as a form of tyranny. A small group (9 per cent of juniors and 13 per cent of seniors) do household tasks for pocket money. A larger group (19 per cent of juniors and 12 per cent of seniors) do so because 'I have to', perhaps without seeing their efforts as meaningful, useful, or companionable. The child who stood out as the most disaffected was a fifth-grader, one of the 4 per cent who reported that they didn't have to do any jobs around the house: 'Why should I? It's their house, not mine'. But the most commonly mentioned negative aspect of doing household jobs was the fact that they simply had to be done.

There is no choice. The sense of not having a choice turns out to have several aspects to it. The first is that you often get the same jobs everyday. No job remains attractive in the face of having to do it every day regardless of how one feels. The task one child sees as attractive is, in the eyes of the child who actually does it every day, a chore. Consider the following comments:

> I wish that every morning I would feed the ducks and goslings instead of what I do.
>
> I wish that I could stay in bed longer. And that I wouldn't do the ducks every day to get them into their pens and feed them.
>
> I wish I could wake up every morning on a farm and feed all the animals and ride horses. That's what I wish I could do. (A city child)
>
> I wish I wouldn't have to feed the horses. (A country child)
>
> I wish I could ride my bike to school.
>
> I wish I didn't have to pump my bike every morning.

'Every day' may also contain the regret that the routine remains the same even when the weather or one's mood changes. It would be nice, the children comment, if on rainy days they did not have to walk the dog or go to swimming training, just as it would be delightful if 'school was cancelled on sunny days'. However, we could take the children's idea of 'every day' with a grain of salt. We often say 'you always' when we mean at best 'most of the time'. This type of exaggeration is clearly reflected in the words of the fifth-grader who said, 'Every day sometimes my brother wakes me up at 6 o'clock'.

A further point of dissatisfaction is that you seldom get to choose which jobs you do or when you do them:

I wish I cold [sic] change my jobs. (Grade 3)

I wish they set the work but we decided when it could be done. (Grade 6)

Furthermore, many jobs are essential duties. They cannot be left undone. We have in mind not jobs like dusting or making one's bed (where there is often room for argument about the necessity of the job) but jobs such as feeding pets, milking cows, or staying with a younger sibling on the way to school. If these are your jobs, there is little room for negotiation about leaving things for another day.

Finally, some jobs are inescapably 'yours'. 'Cleaning up after yourself' seems to be in this category. A specific example is making one's own bed. In many households the 'yours'—'mine' distinction in this area seems to acquire a moral quality, in the sense that it comes to be regarded as wrong or unthinkable to ask others to do them, or as right only if accompanied by a special reason or presented as a request for a special favour, to be returned. Of all the children asked about household jobs, for instance, no child offered a reason for making his or her own bed. Any reason offered related to another's bed: for example, 'I make my brother's bed because he goes to work and doesn't have time'. The particular jobs may vary from family to family, but the recognition that some jobs are 'yours' except for special circumstances apparently starts at an early age.

Is there no way out to all these limits on one's sense of choice? A familiar scene in many households consists of job negotiations over what and when and how much or how well. For what cannot be negotiated, one may fall back on a little fantasy and humour:

I wish I was a Jennie [genie] and help mum and dad because I recon [sic] a mum cant do woke [work]. (Grade 1)

I wish I had magic in my fingers to do all my jobs. (Grade 5)

I wish that in the morning a robot would come and supply our breakfast for us and could make our beds and do all the housework. (Grade 6)

I wish I could just blink and be already dressed and ready for school. (Grade 5)

Getting started in the morning

Getting started on a school day is the second activity in the home setting we have chosen to look at. How is this activity viewed by children?

For a start, we noted that the balance of positive and negative features for this activity is less favourable than it was for doing jobs around the house. Breakfast may be spoken of with enthusiasm. A few children even look forward to the first moments of the day:

I wish that I could wake up early about 6.00 and ride and own my own horse. (Grade 3)

I wish I could get up early and go into the garden and make brefass [*sic*]. (Grade 2)

For the vast majority of children, however, getting started in the morning is an activity with considerable room for improvement. The children's comments bring out a number of features that help account for their views.

Getting started is a transitional activity

Some activities are ends in themselves. You do them for their own sake. They have a purpose, a beginning and an end. Other activities are carried out in order to make a further activity possible. In this sense, they are transitional: a step between one activity and another. Getting started in the morning is transitional, falling between sleep and—on most days—starting school.

There may be times when transitional activities are pleasant—when 'getting there is half the fun'—but these seem to be few. For children, getting started in the morning is not one of them. Why?

One reason is that this moment of transition is not under their control. Someone else usually sets the time when it begins. Someone else may also make the first moment of transition—from sleep to waking—more abrupt than you would wish:

> I wish that my dog would not jump on me and wake me up. (Grade 2)

> I wish that my mother would not come in and wake me up. It would be nicer if the dog did, because he snuggles up to you and mum pulls the bedclothes off and makes you cold. (Grade 5)

> I get up at 8.00 and if I don't get up my brother screams in my ear and I wish he didn't. (Grade 6)

> I wish I could sleep in more because every time I have a dream, when it gets to the good point mum always wakes me up and I can't get the dream back afterwards. (Grade 6)

Also not under their control is the end moment of this transitional step. The children often expressed the wish that school would start later. A few wished that 'school came to me'. The reality, however, is that school has a fixed starting-time and you have to get yourself there.

Time is a pervasive problem

Getting started in the morning might not be such a problem if it were not so firmly tied to the clock. That tie means first of all that you face a lack of match between body time and clock time:

> I wish I could sleep in and get up when I want. (Grade 5)

> I don't like getting out of bed sometimes because you are still tired. (Grade 5)

> I wish I wouldn't have to wake up so early in the morning so I won't get so tied [sic] through the day. (Grade 4)

A further difficulty with clock time is that people feel strongly about it—not only people at home but people at school:

> I wish that if you get up late you don't get told of [off] for being late. (Grade 5)

> I wish when I am late teachers would not make a song and dance about it. (Grade 6)

You may yourself begin to become a little agitated about being 'late':

> I wish I was not late to school all the time. (Grade 3)

I wish a giant came and carried me to school when I'm late (but I am never late!). (Grade 5)

The activities are interlocking

Within a set and fairly inflexible period of time, children need to fit a collection of activities—their own and others. These activities are linked. That is, if one step gets out of place, some changes will have to be made in what follows. As adults, we know this problem well. The children were also well aware that one morning activity affects others:

> I wish I could sleep in and get up when I want. And I wish when I did that I would not have to rush and could still have a big breakfast. (Grade 6)
>
> I wish school started at 10.00 a.m. because I could sleep in. (Grade 3)
>
> I wish a machine could be invented so it would dress me and give me breakfast in tablets so I could get up later. (Grade 5)

The children also make it clear that part of the inter-locking is between your own schedule and that of others. When others fall behind, your morning round has to adjust:

> I wish my dad [who supplies transport] wouldn't sleep in so that I could go to school early and play with my friends. (Grade 2)
>
> I wish not to have to tidy my room and not have to wake my sister up, and also make her get up early so she doesn't make us late. (Grade 5)

These activities concern the timetables and priorities only of people at home. There are, as well, people outside whose time-tables affect yours. The bus has a schedule. So do the people who pick you up or who wait for you to join them.

All this planning and priority-setting might be easier if it took place in a neutral setting. The morning juggle may, in fact, involve a fair level of tension, with the stage managers not in the best of moods or having to resort to strong expressions of feeling in order to get several shows on the road:

> I wish that my family would wake up and everyone would sit down and all have breakfast together, and we would not have to be yelled to school and that we would wake up earlier. (Grade 6)
>
> I wish mum would not growl at me so much. (Grade 4)

I wish that in the morning my mum didn't scream at me and I ate very good things. (Grade 4)

Lost options

The loss of options forms a large part of children's attitudes towards the start of the day. School rules out, as we noted in the preceding chapter, a number of family activities:

When you're at school, you don't see your family. (Grade 3)

You can't really do much with them when you're at school. You can't really talk to them or help them. 'Cause at school you're doing your own work. (Grade 6)

When you're at school, your father is at work and you hardly get to see him. (Grade 4)

I don't get much time to talk with my parents, because I'm always at school. (Grade 5)

In addition, school rules out a number of self-chosen activities for which home is generally the base. The loss is underlined by wishes that:

Instead of going to school I could sleep in my snuggly bed and watch television. (Grade 4)

Not to go to school and I would do nothing for a while. (Grade 4)

I could go down to the creek and fish for a couple of hours. (Grade 5)

I could get up and play for a while instead of having to get ready for school. (Grade 3)

I could have more hours in the morning by myself so that I could do anything I want. (Grade 4)

Working things out: ways of coping with the essentials

In looking at two home activities (household tasks and getting started in the morning, we have concentrated on children's views of what these activities are like), with a special stress on feelings and perceptions of the 'good' and 'not-so-good' parts.

All activities, however, call for some thinking and learning on the part of people involved in them. We made that point in the previous chapter in regard to relationships with family members, asking about the explanations children give for people's behaviour. How do children work out the problems associated with home activities?

We shall outline two areas of mental effort. The first concerns some suggestions for problem-solving: specific ways to soften pressures such as the limited amount of time or choice available. The second concerns an underlying form of learning: particularly when activities form a sequence, we need to learn what comes before what, who is responsible for each part, and what the possibilities are for any switches or substitutions in the scenario.

Easing the pressures

To soften the pressure of limited time, children move quickly to the suggestion: create more time. How might this be done? An occasional child simply wishes to add on hours. In the words of a third-grader, 'I wish we could have about 20 more hours in the morning'. A small number see the solution as lying within themselves ('I wish I could be faster'). The majority, however, see the solution as lying outside themselves, as lying primarily in the way school is organised. As mentioned earlier, many wishes for change in the morning referred to changes associated with school (22 per cent for juniors, 21 per cent for seniors). Almost all of these references concerned a shift in school schedules. Either there should be no school or—far more common—school should start later: at 10.00 a.m., at noon, or after lunch.

Obviously, such 'solutions' are difficult to bring about. What are the more viable alternatives?

One alternative is to inspect again the activities involved, and find out which are 'moveable' or 'squeezable'. What can be moved to another time slot or to another person? What can be dropped out altogether or squeezed so that it takes less time or less effort?

With school ruled out as a moveable or squeezable item, it is the home activities that must come up for such review. One might, for instance, get up earlier, have a shorter shower, get dressed more quickly, run to school rather than walk or—the children's most frequent suggestion—change the nature of breakfast:

I wish I could sleep longer than I do. I wouldn't have to do the
dishes and make my bed. And I would have more time to eat my
breakfast and not have it taken away when I am half-way. (Grade 5)

I wish I could sleep in and not eat breakfast in a rush. (Grade 4)

I wish I'd stay home and watch all the cartoons, then get up, take 5 minutes to eat and go to school. (Grade 5)

I didn't have breakfast. I slept in. (Grade 3)

Children and parents, however, may not agree on what parts of the schedule can be altered or on how the alterations can take place, giving rise perhaps to some unpleasant negotiations. Some parents, for instance, do not perceive breakfast to be as 'squeezable' as their children see it: 'I wish that every morning instead of my mother pushing me to have breakfast, I could fly and be free' (Grade 6). One can readily imagine as well some disagreements on the extent to which showers, morning jobs, or teeth-cleaning can be dropped altogether or given 'a lick and a promise'.

So far the question of malleability has been concerned with activities rather than people. For a number of children, however, time problems in the morning are eased by another person whose schedule is more flexible, who can be asked for assistance. This person is almost always the child's mother, available to help one get dressed, find things and, if time gets completely out of hand, drive you to school. The value of this assistance seems to become apparent to children only when it is removed, as when a mother who has been a full-time homemaker returns to the paid labour force. As a fourth-grader commented: 'I used to be lucky. My mother could always drive me to school and pick me up afterwards if it was rainy'.

The flexibility of mothers and breakfasts is in marvellous contrast to one activity that is almost never nominated for reduction: sleep. The occasional child may wish that 'I could get up an hour earlier—and not be rushed'. The proposal, however, is quickly demolished with the further comment: 'But then I would be so tired'. In the interests of protecting one's hours of sleep, the rest of the morning will have to be pushed and pressed to fit into the time left available.

Learning the script

We have been looking at a particular way of working things out: namely, the problem-solving that results from a particular pressure and takes the form of locating 'moveable' and 'squeezable' parts.

The children's comments also bring out a more general form of thinking and learning that seems to be a regular part of daily life. Among psychologists, this general form of working things out has been labelled 'the learning of scripts'. The original work in this vein dealt with adults and the way they thought about sequences of events, especially sequences—such as going to the dentist or to a restaurant—that were repeated often enought to allow individuals to develop some picture in their heads of the usual order of events. These mental pictures of sequences—these 'scripts' or 'scenarios' —were the essential basis, it was argued, for being able to anticipate events and to plan. The work with adults has been extended to children by Katherine Nelson[2]. It is her work that we draw particular attention to, since she argues that script learning is the basic form of all learning, that it occurs very early in life, and that children put considerable mental effort into learning what comes when. In this respect, her argument is similar to that of Bruner who has emphasised that a great deal of children's learning and thinking is concerned with the development of 'narrative structures'[3].

Getting started on a school day is an activity that clearly calls for learning a script: learning what is fixed and what is optional, what can be moved or squeezed, what can be shifted from one person to another either on a regular basis or as a special favour. The children's comments bring out for us the need for this learning in their daily lives. They also bring out a way of looking at many family negotiations over activities at home. These may well be thought of as negotiations over the questions: Who writes the script? Who can alter it?

Individual differences

As in the previous chapter, we have started with a majority picture and we now wish to consider some individual differences, with the goal again of trying to avoid conventional categorisations.

Ways of working things out

Families, the children suggest, vary in their approaches to home 'scripts'. They vary in what is regarded as a 'proper' script: the right way to do a job or to get started in the morning, the 'possible' and 'impossible' omissions, the degree of squeezing that will be tolerated. They vary also in the way activities are tagged as being the special responsibility of a certain person. In a few families, for instance, the making of one's bed can be someone else's job, set against a majority picture of this being the task most likely to be reported as one's own.

These forms of difference, once we begin to think about them, are familiar from our own experiences of family life and from the comparisons we may make between our own ways of operating and those of other families.

A more subtle form of difference has to do with the attribution of responsibility for any difficulties encountered in activities at home. For most of the children, the source of any problems appears to be external. It lies in school schedules being rigid or in other people sleeping in and 'making you late'. For a much smaller group, the problem lies in themselves. They are 'slow':

> I wish I get up so early and was fast and got to school very early every morning. (Grade 4)
>
> I wish that I could be faster than I usually are. (Grade 2)
>
> I wish I was the fasts [sic] runner in the world so that I could get to school faster. (Grade 4)
>
> I wish that in some way or other I could get a body that was free to do anything with ease. (Grade 5—a child with a physical handicap).

The real problem, in many cases, is not the children's slowness, but the need to fit so much in to so little time, and to match their pace to that of other people.

The pressures of limited time and choice

Feelings of being limited in one's choice of activities and in the amount of time available are widespread. Nevertheless, for some children these pressures seem stronger than for others. What contributes to such variations?

One factor is the availability of options. We are all aware of differences among families in the extent to which there are options for leaving jobs undone, for asking someone else to do them, or for deciding when a job can be done. A second factor is the nature of one's tasks. Limited choice is undoubtedly a different matter for jobs that are easily seen as essential than it is for those where the necessity is less comprehensible. It does make immediate sense that animals have to be fed or that wood must be gathered for the kitchen fire: more so than wiping off dust or vacuuming a room.

Factors that contribute to differences in the sense of time pressure turn out to be somewhat different. One is the number of activities to be fitted together. There seems to be a world of difference in the demand for time planning between the children who list only one job ('I make my bed') and those who have many:

Get the wood for the fire, bring the washing in, feed the animals. (Grade 5)

The beds, collect the laundry—well, half of it—stack the dishes and take the garbage out. (Grade 4)

Take the clothes off the line, do the garbage bin, burn the papers, feed the cat, set the table, help in the kitchen. (Grade 4)

I cut the wood, get the sticks and the wood, and help mum make beds and do the washing up, and feed the dog and cat. (Grade 5)

I wash the dishes, I clean the table, I clean my room, I sweep the house and I feed the pigs, feed the chickens, feed the pigeons. And we've got little baby chicks. I feed them and I water the lawn. (Grade 4)

Another factor has to do with the time available. This may become short either because you cannot bring yourself to get up earlier, or because there is a long distance between house and school. The time available for morning activities, for instance, is theoretically greater for children who 'just step out the door and cross the road to school', than for children whose travel time is long. Many of the children (43 per cent) turned out to be within walking distance of school. For some, however, the distance is long. Consider, for instance, a country fifth-grader:

I ride my bike to school. It takes about an hour and a half.

Or a sixth-grader who travels for two hours in order to come into the city to attend a particular private school:

My mother drives me to the station and it takes about two hours to get to X and I change trains and I walk from that stop to school.

A final factor is the nature of the people you need to coordinate with. It is one thing, for instance, to walk (you can always go a little faster) and another to have to count on an unreliable transport system. The problem may be either urban or rural, but the most memorable example comes from a country area:

> I sometimes miss the bus because on Tuesday it is supposed to come to Kangy Angy and the bus driver seems to forget.

Although we have consciously tried to avoid the conventional ways of categorising children, we feel it is useful here to draw attention to a comparison between country and city children—in terms of the number and function of their jobs. Country children are likely to have more jobs, and their activities seem to be more obviously essential to the daily workings of their home environment. They also seem to have a greater degree of time pressure associated with longer distances between home and school, and fewer opportunities for amending the situation if something goes wrong. To miss the one and only bus, or to have the bus driver 'forget', is less likely in the city. There are, of course, city children who have many household jobs and a complex route to school, but it appears that those in the country generally have greater demands placed on them in these areas of activity.

A change of scene

So far we have dealt with family life in terms of relationships among people, and household activities. It is time to shift to another setting: that of school. We have had ample opportunity to note the validity of a point made by Bronfenbrenner[4] about settings: namely, that what happens in one alters what happens in another. For all that the two settings are linked, however, children do not view the two in the same light. We shall turn, then, to the setting of school, looking again at relationships with people—teachers, in particular—and then at activities—this time in the classroom.

3
LIFE AT SCHOOL:
teachers

School may seem a place where teachers evaluate children. The reverse is just as much the case. Children regularly compare notes about teachers. Like experienced travellers, they tell each other about schools and teachers they have encountered:

> This school is O.K. I've been to some worse ones. (Grade 5)
>
> I had a teacher once in Mullingimbie and he was good. (Grade 4)

The evaluations start early and have many bases:

> Mr G. is a good teacher. He gives us sport. (Grade 2)
>
> They are good when they have time for you. (Grade 3)
>
> They have to understand the way that you think and be patient with us. (Grade 5)
>
> Someone with humour and someone with understanding. The kind of person who will understand you and doesn't get angry when you don't get it straight away. (Grade 6)
>
> I like a teacher that have feelings with their children. (Grade 6)
>
> I think the teacher should be able to get along with the children and should enjoy their work as much as the children who enjoy their work. And don't accuse until they find out what really happened. (Grade 6)

How does all this evaluation come about? What lies behind the qualities children look for, the features they note as 'good' and 'not-so-good'?

Part of the background is that children are indeed like travellers or voyagers. They make a major move from being 'at home' to being 'at school' and then continue to change regularly from one school grade to another. In this respect, they are like adults who regularly change jobs, houses or countries. With each change, they do not come to the new environment empty-handed. They bring the physical baggage of books, pencils, notes and bits and pieces from home, odd souvenirs from past years. More importantly, they bring—like every voyager—a set of *expectations*. These colour the experience of school and teachers. When the expectations are favourably met, everything is labelled 'good'. When the reality does not compare favourably, the response is one of disappointment, frustration and sometimes anger.

We shall be singling out three main hopes and expectations associated with school. First, there is the expectation that you are going to learn, and the teacher will make it possible: 'They give you education', to use a first-grader's comment. It is also hoped that the teacher will be human and friendly. He or she, in the words of a sixth-grader, should 'be a person, not a policeman'. Then, there is the expectation that you will be an accepted member of the class, and be respected at least as much as anyone else. Classrooms are large groups, and the problems of rivalry are even more complex than they are in families. A child generally wants to be noticed by the teacher and at the same time be an accepted member of your peer group, not a 'teacher's pet'. He or she usually hopes for at least 'equal' treatment.

A further part of the background to children's views is the special position of teachers in relation to children. In the children's eyes—and in reality—teachers have a great deal of power. They are score-keepers (and the score is often embarrassingly public). They are gatekeepers, controlling access to many of the good things one wants: knowledge, skills, good feelings about oneself, a reputation as competent, time 'outside'. Moreover, the relationship between children and their teacher is not like that between children and their parents. With parents, one may feel there is an obligation to regard you as 'special' and to 'look after you all your life'. With parents, one may expect to be accepted, just 'because I'm me' or because 'I'm all they have'. Not so with teachers. Under these circumstances, a somewhat different set of expectations applies and a different bill of rights needs to be negotiated. As we shall see, one frequent reaction is to turn 'constitutional lawyer', proposing many a rule for fair and proper treatment.

Most of the material under discussion in this chapter comes from the question: 'What makes a good teacher?' Comments about teachers also appeared in answers to some other questions: 'If you could change one thing about school, what would you change?'; 'What do you like about school?'; 'Is there anything you don't like?'. Among wishes for change, teachers are the subject of 9 per cent of the juniors' wishes (most wishes deal with activities: changes in what is learned and when). Teachers also appear briefly on the lists of what is liked about school (2 per cent and 3 per cent, respectively, of the juniors' and the seniors' remarks). However, they are more prominent on the lists of what is disliked (12 per cent of juniors' comments, 24 per cent of seniors').

Table 3.1   The main qualities mentioned by children from all grades in their definitions of a good teacher, parent, and friend (shown as the percentage of all qualities mentioned)

	teacher	parent	friend
	%	%	%
A caring attitude			
Loves, cares for, comforts you	14	27	23
Provides material things	—	6	—
Protects/looks after you	—	6	?
Does not hit/fight	4	4	4
Controls, but fairly	8	11	—
Total	26	54	27
Understanding and sharing			
Makes you feel special	5	8	22
Understands you	10	8	6
You understand them	8	2	6
Shares fun with you	6	3	19
Shares things with you	—	—	6
Total	29	21	59
Helping to opening up the world			
Gives access to people and places	9	9	2
Teaches, explains, shows	28	4	1
Total	37	13	3

Note: We have omitted all qualities that account for 2 per cent or less of those mentioned.

Incidentally, the latter figures seem to suggest that children's feelings about teachers become increasingly negative as they proceed through school.

Suppose we ask first: *Are good teachers the same as good parents?* They are both adults, and perhaps children extend the same expectations to one group as to the other. The answer to that question is: only partly. We have brought together in one table (Table 3.1) the main features mentioned for good parents and good teachers (as well as good friends, anticipating part of Chapter 5). This table tells us that the main function of parents is to care for you, while the main function of teachers is to open up the world by teaching, explaining, showing you 'how'. The table tells us also that teachers are nonetheless not expected to be simply teaching machines. It is important to children that teachers care for them and understand them. The need for teachers to understand you (10 per cent of all comments on good teachers) is in fact higher than it is for parents (8 per cent). Teachers differ from parents, however, in the importance of you understanding them (8 per cent for teachers, 2 per cent for parents): a sign, perhaps, that children do not always regard teachers' behaviour as making sense.

Next we look at the question: *Do the children's opinions on the qualities of a good teacher change much from the early to the later grades?* That question is answered in Table 3.2.

Table 3.2   Changes by grade in the main qualities mentioned in definitions of a good teacher (shown as the percentage of all qualities mentioned)

	All grades	Grades 1 & 2	Grades 3 & 4	Grades 5 & 6
Loves, cares for, comforts you	14	17	19	11
Does not hit/fight	4	5	5	4
Controls, but fairly	8	4	7	9
Makes you feel special	5	5	4	6
Understands you	10	4	7	13
You understand them	8	10	8	8
Shares fun with you	6	5	5	7
Gives access to people and places	9	14	11	7
Teaches, explains, shows	28	28	31	27

Briefly, the differences across grades are not striking. The children seem to have a fairly consistent picture of what the role of teacher should cover. At all grades, they agree that their primary task is to teach well. One difference that occurs is a decline in the importance of teachers looking after you, being comforting and sympathetic. This general need for caring drops from 17 per cent and 19 per cent among the younger children to 11 per cent among those in Grade 5 and 6, who presumably feel more able to stand on their own feet. The decline is offset by an increase over the grades in the importance given to the fair exercise of control and discipline (4 per cent, 7 per cent, 9 per cent) and to being understood (4 per cent, 7 per cent, 13 per cent). These are small differences, however. The most notable feature is the similarity of definition across grades. The children seem to come to school with expectations already in mind.

Hopes, expectations, and reality

We mentioned in the first section of the chapter three main hopes and expectations that children bring to their relationships with teachers.

We shall look at each of these expectations in turn, exploring the way children see them and give meaning to them.

The teacher will make learning possible

Bear in mind that most children see teachers as not only important to the learning process, but indispensable:

> They give you education. (Grade 2)

> She tells us things we don't know and we learn when we grow up. If there are no teachers, we would have to grow up and we wouldn't know anything. (Grade 3)

Only among seniors do we find a few doubting the necessity for teachers:

> Wish we had a computer as teacher. Then he would not throw chalk and also would not give us so much homework. (Grade 6)

> Wish we have a robot which could walk and talk and give us no homework. (Grade 6)

Wish we didn't have teachers and the kids could swap ideas.
(Grade 5)

In all, there are only six such comments (one concerning peer-teaching, five mentioning computers). More of this type of comment might emerge if one were to ask directly, 'Are teachers necessary?' What we do have, however, are many gratuitous comments about how necessary teachers are.

What exactly are teachers expected to do? Primarily, they are expected to show you how or—to adopt a phrase used many times by children—to 'explain'. The flavour of the children's expectations is brought out for us by comments such as these, referring to 'good' and 'poor' methods:

> If you don't understand something, she'll keep explaining it to you. She won't just say 'You haven't been listening'. She'll keep on explaining until you get it. (Grade 6)

> I'd like to have a teacher like we had last year ... if you didn't understand something, she'd explain it very carefully. (Grade 5)

> I like how kind they are and how much they teach you, and it is really good when they go over it to make sure that we know it. And some teachers just put it on the board, like Mr N. in fourth grade. (Grade 5)

> She doesn't say 'Open the textbook to page 68' or something, and she doesn't read the book or something while you do it. She writes it up on the board and she goes round to people who don't understand. (Grade 6)

> They don't just say 'Right, it is on the board, and get it all right', and they make sure that everybody understands—and they help you if you don't. (Grade 6)

So far we have talked about the expectation that learning will proceed in a successful fashion and that teachers will be able to 'explain' everything. Sooner or later, however, difficulties will be encountered. What is then likely to occur? One consequence is that children will simply cease to like school or to approve of teachers. Some children, however, look to themselves as the critical factor:

> I wish I could always be right at school. (Grade 2)

> I wish I was a good worker. (Grade 1)

More often, they look for causes in the teacher. The teacher has not explained things in the right way, or often enough. The teachers' views, of course, are likely to be in different terms and we shall have occasion to see that the children are well aware of these. We shall cite at this stage only one illustrative comment:

> When you stand up and ask questions, she says, 'You weren't listening; go back to your desk and figure it out'. (Grade 5)

The teacher will be human and friendly

The importance of this expectation is brought to light by the number of times that 'the good teacher' is defined in terms of feelings. Good teachers will understand you, be sympathetic, share a few jokes with you, make good sense to you.

What exactly do children expect? One component is patience and sympathy:

> They are good when they have time for you. (Grade 2)
>
> I like the way they are nice to you if you are hurt or anything and nobody will play with you. (Grade 4)
>
> I like a teacher that if somebody's crying, I reckon they should comfort you but they shouldn't butt in to other people's business. (Grade 5)
>
> I like a teacher that have feelings with their children. And sometimes, something's wrong, and wouldn't press on them if something's wrong because it will make them bad. Politeness, humour, understanding, and most inner feeling. (Grade 6)

There are other qualities which children appreciate:

> I like it when Ben H. makes fun of the teacher and the teacher smiles at him. (Grade 2)
>
> ... gives a bit of a joke now and then. (Grade 6)
>
> Sometimes Mr K. is good because he is sort of funny. Like the other day. I am in our Christmas concert doing a tap dance and I was showing it to my friend, Elizabeth. And he comes over behind me and he sort of pulled faces and everything, and Elizabeth saw him and I didn't. (Grade 5)
>
> Good teachers, like Mr W. You can sit down and talk to him a lot. And sometimes he does things. Like yesterday afternoon, I was at the bus stop and he said 'Goodbye Joanna'. (Grade 5)

Other comments show that children do not like being ignored or treated in a detached manner by their teacher:

Like our teacher, outside he talks to the gardener, and like I said, he should stay with his class. (Grade 6)

If you're playing outside in the garden, they should join in with you. (Grade 4)

Once again, these expectations are not always met. The children encounter teachers who are 'kind' and teachers who are 'crabby', who 'yell' or 'scream', 'get bad moods real quickly', 'throw chalk', 'hit', and act like 'policemen'. They also, inevitably, encounter penalties. They will not themselves always be 'good' and their departures from perfection will draw some kind of controlling reaction from teachers: from 'quiet talks' and writing lines to 'being told off', kept in, sent to the principal's office, or caned.

What is likely to occur under these circumstances? One consequence is that children come to like some teachers rather than others, and to judge some as better than others. Once again, they look for explanations. In addition, they show a strong interest in working out the rules and working out what is fair. The mental work is particularly pronounced when they need to reconcile the expectation that the teacher will be in charge ('They should be strict', 'They should not let kids do just anything') with the expectation that they will also be human and friendly. We shall soon be looking at this dilemma in more detail, concentrating on the rules children propose for how penalties should be administered. A few comments will give a brief foretaste of the children's proposals:

A strict teacher makes a good one because then they can control the students, and they should have a good sense of humour with the kids and have fun with them. (Grade 6)

Good teachers don't throw fits and chuck mentals and things. (Grade 5)

A good teacher . . . If they are mad about something, they shouldn't take it out on you. (Grade 6)

If one person is stupid, they shouldn't keep the whole class in. (Grade 5)

You will be an accepted member of the class

School, office, factory: these settings involve larger groups than encountered in the home. They present the individual with the possibility of not being known, even by name. To have someone say 'Goodbye, Joanna' is a sign that one is known. One may, especially at first in a large group, feel faceless, lost in the crowd. Small wonder that children sometimes have the type of feelings expressed by one fourth-grader:

> I wish I was the only person in the playground, and that the teachers thought I was the greatest person in the world.

Children may also wish that—if they cannot be special—at least their individual needs will be known:

> A good teacher is an understanding teacher, so she understands all your problems: why can't you do this, and can't do that. (Grade 4)

> A good teacher will not press on you when she knows you're having troubles at home. (Grade 6)

The reality is that teachers often do not know their children as individuals. Reasonable or not, the fact is that although teachers and pupils spend long days together, each child has to share a teacher's time, attention, affection, warmth and respect. You cannot be the only one in a class. Sharing must take place.

What is likely to occur under such circumstances? As with siblings—but perhaps even more so—the children argue that if all cannot be 'special' then none should be. Everyone must be given 'fair' treatment. In the forceful words of a sixth-grader:

> ... a teacher should not show her likes and dislikes and press all her hate on one and shove them off where they can't see the board properly, and put her little pets in the front where they can see everything and give them all the nice jobs. A teacher should be able to give everybody a chance to try out their best and not to say which one looks the best.

Several fifth-graders echo the same theme:

> I don't like the teacher because when she gets stamps, she always gives it to the same person every time, and it's not fair.

> [Some teachers] tend to pick on people and they usually have one or two pets that they give things to and do things with more than the other kids.

> I wish we had more teachers that were fair to you, and to everyone else.

Working things out: explanations for classroom events

How do people come to terms with hopes and expectations that are not met? In all areas of daily life, one way of working things out is to find causes: reasons for one's successes and problems, health or illness, happy or unhappy interactions with others. In psychologists' terms, we make attributions about behaviour or events.

What are the events or behaviour patterns that children work at finding explanations for? Two stand out: situations where the children are having trouble learning, and times when the teachers are angry, 'grumpy', 'moody' or 'unfriendly'.

Explanations for learning problems

The children's most frequent explanation is in terms of the teachers. They 'don't explain'. They don't 'explain it properly', 'explain it so you can do it', or 'explain it enough times'.

Why do teachers 'not explain'? Sometimes the children are aware that their teachers place the blame on them:

> He puts a new fraction on the board and we don't know how to do it. And when we put up our hand to ask, he says 'You should know that by now'. (Grade 5)

> I don't like Mr ... He tells you 'Fold your arms' and when you're folding your arms, he says I'm dreaming, and I'm not dreaming. Well, maths I don't really like and he gives you hard divide. (Grade 5)

> Most times if you put up your hand to ask something—if you get stuck on a sum or something—when he says 'yes', he ends up blowing you up and say 'You don't listen'. (Grade 5)

> And there's another thing I don't like about him. He said that if you ever want help, well you should put up your hand and ask the teacher. And one day I put up my hand and asked the teacher and he just said, 'Oh you never listen, do you'. (Grade 5)

> I wish that teachers wouldn't get quite so angry, and would help you out with your problems and not say 'Go back and use your brain'. (Grade 4)

An occasional child accepts the teachers' refusal to explain—at least for a second time—and sees the refusal as for the child's own good:

A good teacher gets cranky if you keep getting it wrong, because she doesn't like to see you get it wrong. She likes to see you be able to do it, and be able to do it for high school, so that—you know—you are not just sitting around saying 'I can't do it, will you please help me?'. (Grade 5)

A kindly explanation is also offered by an interviewer at the end of a string of complaints, but not accepted by the children. The fourth fifth-grader in a row complains about teachers not 'showing you how':

I reckon they have to explain more things to you. And these days all the teachers hardly explain all the things to you.

Do you think they don't have enough time?

No, they've got time.

Most of the children are readily indignant at the suggestion that they 'don't listen', 'dream', 'don't use their brains', or 'aren't trying'. They cling firmly to the belief that 'explaining' is the teacher's job:

I like the teachers if they understand. Like if maybe you can't do something and they will explain how to do it, and if you can't get it they don't go mad at you. 'Cause it is their fault really, 'cause they don't explain it properly. (Grade 5)

What explanations are left, then, for the teachers not explaining properly? A few children in the upper grades define a good teacher as someone who is 'brainy' and 'knows what they're talking about', implying that some teachers may explain poorly because of lack of ability. This type of explanation, however, is rare. These primary school children accept that teachers have the knowledge. The problem is that for some mysterious reason, teachers 'won't explain'. In the words of a fifth-grader:

I hate maths, because our teacher doesn't explain it to you. She says, 'Just try it'. And you just can't do it because you just don't know how to do it, and you just don't understand it. And the teachers *won't explain* it to you. And even when they do explain it, you get more confused.

All told, the children are describing a tug-of-war between teachers and children for the explanation of any difficulties in learning. Each side appears to choose the explanation that puts it in the best light, probably having more understanding of the other's position than is willingly admitted. What is maintained, on the one hand, is the right to have something explained one more time, and—on the other—the right to be listened to when one does explain.

Within the tug-of-war, there appears also to be a difference in the use of words. The children use the term 'explain' or 'explained properly' until they have understood it. Given this use of the word, it makes little sense for the teacher to say 'I have explained it', meaning 'to my satisfaction'. We suspect that not only children use words with such different shades of meaning. 'Why didn't you tell me?' 'I've told you several times.' That is a familiar exchange at many ages.

Explanations for teachers' negative behaviour

Teachers clearly are not always friendly. Even allowing for some exaggeration in the children's phrasing, teachers are often perceived as 'angry'. In the children's words, they 'yell', 'scream', 'throw fits', 'chuck mentals', 'blow you up', 'do their blocks', 'do their nanas', 'throw chalk', 'hit you', 'bash you'.

What are children to make of such behaviour? Part of working things out consists of drawing a distinction between angry behaviour when they have misbehaved (when they have done something 'really wrong'), and angry behaviour when they have simply not understood something. It is the second type of anger that the children find puzzling and object to.

Anger when you 'don't know something' or 'haven't understood' is a major issue. Again and again, one hears comments on this puzzling aspect of teachers:

> A good teacher...She likes to be around children. And she tries to understand what the children...Like when Adam did a '4' and did a back to front four, she wouldn't scream. (Grade 3)

> I wish the teachers would help us when we get something wrong instead of scolding us. (Grade 4)

> I like a teacher who isn't cross when she doesn't understand you. (Grade 5)

> I don't like it when you don't understand something and they explain it to you, but you still don't understand it, and then they get really angry. (Grade 6)

I wish the teachers wouldn't get quite so angry and would help you with your problems and not say 'Go back and use your brains'. (Grade 4)

I like it when they don't yell at you all the time. They do things calmly and go through them slowly and if you don't know it, or couldn't hear properly, they don't blow your head off. (Grade 6)

I like when teachers don't shout at you, and if you get a project and you get a bad mark they don't say 'Get out of here' or something like that. They say 'Try next time'. (Grade 6)

How do children account for such behaviour? Some of the accounts—as they were for teachers not 'explaining'—are in terms of it being for the children's own good:

If you be naughty and the teacher has to growl at you, he doesn't want to, but he has to because he wants you to learn. (Grade 2)

I reckon that it is good in a way that she gets cranky because you try harder to get it right. (Grade 5)

You might be cranky about something and the teacher yells and you might not want to do any more work and the teacher yells at you and you go back to doing your work. (Grade 5)

If we didn't get told off, we'd probably be like those guys that go around who haven't learned anything. They kill people and things like that. (Grade 6)

An occasional child sees the problem as lying in the children. In the words of a fourth-grader:

They are good when they have good students to make them happy.

Most of the explanations, however, have to do with the nature of teachers. The fault may lie in their dispositions, experiences or age:

They have no patience. (Grade 4)

... has some children of her own so that they know how to teach them, and so they can teach us. (Grade 5)

A good teacher is someone who is pretty young so they can remember what they went through at school. So they know how the kid feels. (Grade 6)

It is only the seniors who expressed the notion that it is not part of human nature or daily life to be forever friendly and courteous. These kind comments, like those that see angry behaviour as for the children's good, are again referring only to being 'told off' in words:

> It is just that people are bossy sometimes, and sometimes something must be wrong with them, and they don't know they are really rousing on you, and they are pretending sometimes. (Grade 5)

> Sometimes they've had a bad night and are feeling crabby. (Grade 6)

> When you come to school, you're with friends most of the day. And teachers do get a bit bossy sometimes. But you have to give them sometimes to be in a bad mood. (Grade 6)

Such tolerant ways of working things out are not offered for stronger forms of anger on the part of the teachers—which are not frequent. Most of the children see teachers' anger as a teacher's problem, and account for it on the grounds that they are not 'good' teachers.

Working things out: rules for teaching

In previous sections on working things out, we have noted three lines of thought that are prominent in the children's comments. One has to do with observing how things are done: 'learning the script' is the phrase we have used in the description of getting started in the morning. A second has to do with developing explanations: for sibling friction, for parents' behaviour and now for why one is not learning or why teachers are grumpy. A third line of thought concerns ideas and proposals for change, reform, or improvement. This line of thought emerged in comments on what good parents should do, and in the problem-solving approach to improving the start of the day.

Proposals for reform or improvement are prominent in comments on teachers. More so than for parents, children sprinkle their comments on teachers with references to 'should' and 'ought'. These references are especially frequent in discussions of how teachers should teach, and how they should control a class or respond to misdeeds.

We have brought the many comments together in the form of 'rules' proposed by children. These rules serve several functions.

They make it possible to judge teachers, sorting them into the 'good', the 'not so good', and the 'awful'. They also make possible conversations among children: conversations based on agreement or disagreement among themselves, adding to the store of gossip and information about the teachers' good and bad points, their foibles and their moods. Children clearly spend a great deal of time commenting on teachers and comparing them with one another. Finally, the 'rules' appear to serve as a basis for negotiations with teachers. To the extent that teachers and children agree on the rules that teachers should follow, children can argue that certain ways of proceeding are not 'fair' and may succeed in having a task or a penalty changed. They may also, it has been proposed, feel justified in being 'unruly' or 'disorderly' when they feel teachers are refusing to negotiate or to follow 'reasonable' unwritten rules.[1]

In this section we shall consider the rules children propose for teachers assigning tasks. Overall, the children's comments amount to proposing that teachers should follow five rules. We might easily extend the same set to any work setting: home, office, or factory.

They should make the work possible. In the children's comments, this appears particularly in the form of saying that teachers, when they set work, should also show you how to do it. They should, to repeat that much-used word, 'explain' it. In essence:

> She tells you, makes you understand, doesn't just say 'Hey, do it'. (Grade 5)

They should allow a reasonable amount of time for the job. Three comments will serve as an example:

> They should give you enough time. You really can't keep up at anything. (Grade 3)

> I like teachers that help you a lot and they give you time to finish your work. They don't kind of rush it and say 'Do this' and then you're on to the next thing. If they teach us like that, everyone will get their work done. (Grade 3)

> They give you one work and they give you so much time to do it and take out another book and you feel worried that you won't get it done. (Grade 5)

They should pay some attention to your state and to the time of day. Good teachers give you breaks when you are tired. They also do not give you the hardest job when you are least fresh.

> Good teachers give you a break in your work and let your arms rest. (Grade 6)

> You come in after big lunch and you're really hot and sweaty and the teacher comes in and says 'Get out your social studies'. And she writes all that writing on the board and you don't want to do it, and if you don't do it you get into trouble, and you get very tired. (Grade 4)

They should keep work within school hours. This rule emerged in discussions about homework and about work taking over times considered as times for rest, play, sport or talk.

> I don't like teachers who make you do things after the hooter has gone and you are supposed to be on free time. (Grade 6)

> And some teachers give you a lot of work, especially homework when that's the time for rest from school. (Grade 6)

They should allow some choice and variety. This rule is prominent in comments on work that is 'boring' and in the wishes for activities and topics that are of the children's choice:

> Why can't there be some time when we do what we want to do? (Grade 6)

> They should let us decide sometimes. (Grade 5)

> I wish teachers would let us set some of our own work.

> I wish teachers would trust us. (Grade 6)

They should keep track of work that is done, and recognise good work. In the words of an aggrieved fifth-grader:

> I hate it when you're told to do something and you've already done it. And then you get into trouble for not doing it and you get into trouble for not doing anything.

Keeping track also means keeping track for the class, in the form of not setting tests on work not covered (a grievance expressed strongly, but only by a few children).

Recognition of good work is a subtler issue. One suspects it is always an implicit rule, but the explicit references to it are mainly from juniors, perhaps because seniors have learned that an open interest in praise or reward is not acceptable behaviour. In the juniors' comments, teachers are 'good' when:

You do maths right and they tell you you're good. (Grade 2)

You do good work sometimes and they give you stickers. (Grade 3)

When this theme is mentioned by seniors, the phrasing is somewhat more subtle:

A good teacher should praise you when you are trying. (Grade 5)

They should let the people go that are being good. Like Mr O., our new teacher. I cleaned up my desk and I was the first one standing and he let me go. (Grade 5)

Working things out: rules for control and discipline

It is in this area that proposals for how things should be done are especially marked. The children's comments bring out three points. First, they see some form of control as necessary. Second, they seek some form of balance between control and harshness: 'strict but not too strict', 'soft but not too soft'. Third, they have in mind a specific set of rules that define proper forms of control. Let us take these points in order, giving most space to the rules themselves.

Children expect teachers to set limits on some activities, to establish rules, and to maintain a climate in which the activities of the day can proceed fairly efficiently and amicably. They may complain about 'too many rules' but they do not expect teachers to abdicate control. A teacher who is too 'soft' is not regarded with favour. 'If she was soft, you wouldn't learn anything' says a fifth-grader. 'A bad teacher will let you do anything', says another. Nor should a teacher yield too easily to the children's pressure. As some fourth-graders put it:

I think that a teacher is maybe sometimes too soft on you so that you might want her to let you off and not do your work, and she gets upset at you because you have to learn, and people might think she is a nice teacher when she is just soft.

A good teacher should not let you get away with things.

Further, a good teacher should not appear to plead ineffectively. In a sixth-grader's cutting description:

If we talk, then she comes out and says: 'Now you must learn, children. You must be good and responsible—and don't talk. And your manners must be nice'. And we're getting sick of it and everything, and the boys, they get restless, and they get in more trouble, and they pretend they can't hear her.

The children argue for a balance, for a mixture of properties that may seem originally incompatible. 'Strict but not all that strict', 'stern but kind', 'reasonable strict but lets you have fun as well', 'strict but not too strict and she should be fair': these are phrases expressing the need for mixed qualities. 'Close but not buddy-buddy', 'soft and hard', are others. The search for the right mixture can tie one in verbal knots. Witness a fourth-grader:

> I reckon half and half of everything. He should be strict sometimes but then again he should be a little bit not strict.

To help clarify what is meant by such statements we will look at some of the children's opinions on the type of rules good teachers should follow.

They should not punish the whole group. For example:

> Some teachers. . . one person is stupid so they keep the whole class in as well. (Grade 5)

> If one person mucks up, he gets cranky at the whole class and then he sets us lots of homework. (Grade 6)

> Like someone talks when he wants silence, or while he is working out his estimates or something. And he punishes the whole class. And sometimes he knows who the person is who was talking but yet he punishes the whole class. (Grade 6)

Such comments suggest that group punishment has some legal sub-clauses. It seems to become worse if most (or all but one) of the class is innocent and if the real culprit is known or suspected (that is, the teacher does not make the effort to identify the one for the benefit of the rest). Interesting also is the scarcity of comment on group punishment being avoided by the children naming the guilty party. In all the comments on group penalties, we encountered only one suggestion of pressure on a child to 'admit it' so that a class would not be denied an excursion. Honour at this level seems to require suffering in silence, and one wonders when this type of unspoken rule might ever be broken.

They should not punish the wrong person. For example:

> Well, some things I don't like about school is that if your friend starts talking to you, well the teacher says, 'Hey, were you talking?'

and you get sent out and that's the part that's not really fair. (Grade 6)

The innocent party, however, need not be oneself:

Like Barry C. Sometimes some boys push him over and he gets into trouble instead of the other boys. They rumble him in the classroom and sometimes the teacher stands him in the corner instead of the other boys. (Grade 5)

There is this boy and often he gets into trouble, but even when he doesn't, Mr W. jumps on him.

Punishing the wrong person meets special disapproval if the teacher is perceived as taking little effort to locate the culprit:

When Mr C. is out in his storeroom, a lot of people talk. And he comes in. The first person he sees, he picks on. (Grade 5)

I think teachers should have the right to belt people. But if he doesn't really have any proof of them doing the wrong thing, I think he usually blames it on the same person that did it before. (Grade 3)

They're good when they don't jump to conclusions. (Grade 6)

I think a good teacher should be able to understand and look into a person's point of view. Like some teachers just look at them and think that just because they've got a bad reputation, they've done something wrong. But they should look into their point of view and see what the person's thinking to see if she's guilty or not. (Grade 6)

They should give equal punishment for equal wrongs. This idea is expressed in remarks such as these:

A guy in our class, he gets into trouble. But he *really* gets into trouble. The other boy, he does things just as bad but he doesn't. Our teacher doesn't really do much about it. (Grade 5)

They should not shame people. The sharpest comment comes from a group of fifth-graders discussing what they dislike about teachers (a long and lively discussion). The remark is in terms that seem to reflect first-hand experience:

I don't like when the teacher gives you a smack. And when you can't answer a question, they make you stand up and say it. Like Mr W., he makes you stand up and say 'I am a fool' five times. (Grade 5)

Physical punishment also elicits concern about shaming. It is not only that children object to certain penalties when they are themselves the target. They also object to the public nature of the penalty, both when they are the watchers and the one being watched:

> I don't like to see people getting into trouble. (Grade 3)
>
> I don't like seeing people get the strap. (Grade 6)
>
> I don't like it when the teacher gives you the ruler and all the kids are watching and you're not thinking of anything except that it hurts a lot. (Grade 6)

They should not use physical punishment. This comment appears at many grade levels:

> I wish people wouldn't get the cuts. (Grade 3)
>
> I don't like it when my friends get the strap or get into trouble. (Grade 4)
>
> I don't like getting smacked. (Grade 3)
>
> . . .getting into trouble and getting the strap. (Grade 3)
>
> When they punish you, it shouldn't be physical hurt. It should be something like staying after school. (Grade 6)
>
> They've even got a strap which is a piece of leather and it hurts you on your hand and it goes numb. (Grade 6)
>
> I'd rather get detention after school, then you don't cry. (Grade 6)
>
> When Mr J. gets angry, I think he's going to give me the cane, and you get all upset about it. Sometimes you get really angry and in a fighting mood. (Grade 5)

As a disliked feature of school, physical punishment is singled out for specific mention by 3 per cent of juniors and 7 per cent of seniors, a fairly high rating when one considers the large number of possible topics that can be mentioned. But opinions can vary a little on physical punishment. An example is a group of sixth-graders in a coeducational school discussing the features of a 'good' teacher. They offered proposals for several kinds of pen-alty: picking up papers, doing extra work, or getting the cane. The last of these divided the group. 'Fair if you do something real bad', said one, 'Only for a big reason, not a little one', said another. Ineffective, said a third: 'Sometimes a person gets it too often and they get used to it and it doesn't hurt them' (an interesting argument in terms of effect rather than justice). A different note was sounded by one sixth-grader who disliked 'the way people get the cane' and added that 'they shouldn't be getting the cane because they [teachers] aren't responsible for the children, the parents are'. Overall, the comments on physical punishment are disapproving, and often heart-wrenching. One empathises with the last child quoted. By what right do teachers act in this way?

Proposals for fair penalties

All forms of penalty attract some negative comments. Being caned or hit hurts physically. Being yelled at makes you upset. Being kept in means that you lose free time. Being sent out makes you 'feel lonely'.

What do the children suggest? A number approve of being *'talked to quietly'*. Several point to the importance of being given *warnings* and *progressive penalties*, but not empty threats. Others point to the value of *individualising* penalties:

> Sometimes she doesn't smack you, and gives you a quiet talk if you've done something wrong. (Grade 2)

> She keeps you in at lunch and talks to you for a long minute. (Grade 3)

> A good teacher gives you a warning before you get in trouble. (Grade 5)

> Mr F. is good in a way because he gives you about five warnings, and he writes in his diary. As soon as you do anything, he doesn't go off his block. (Grade 5)

> I reckon the first time you should get told off, and if you do it again, you should maybe get 100 lines. (Grade 5)

> A good teacher is usually...You do it once and they say 'Don't do it again 'cause I will give you an imposition'. So you do it again and they give you another imposition of a hundred words. And do it again and she will double it and keep on doubling it until it gets to about 200 words. And then if you do it again, she won't double it. She will say, 'Come to the office', and get the stick. And then you deserve it anyway. (Grade 5)

> I think teachers, when they make a threat, they should carry it out. Don't just say it. Because this boy in our class, he's always getting warnings, but the warnings are never carried out on him. (Grade 5)

> Something you like to do—if you are naughty, he doesn't let you do it. (Grade 2)

Not the cane. Some people prefer to go on excursions. And if they really like to go on excursions and they don't go: that's a really bad punishment for them. (Grade 5)

Some children seemed to be proposing that the punishment should fit the crime:

I like the teacher if she doesn't throw a fit at you if you accidentally do something. (Grade 5)

I don't like getting into trouble for nothing. (Grade 3)

I think teachers should be considerate. I mean sort of not like our second class teacher...She kept slapping people on the bottom and things like that, and I don't think people should do that unless it's necessary. (Grade 5)

We might say that the children are arguing for the need to temper power with justice, and justice with compassion and perhaps even a little humour.

Last year we had a teacher and he was really good. He understood us and he used to sort of play games with us. Like if someone was naughty he used to make us bend over and he used to pretend to smack us but he didn't. But we used to have talking time and we used to talk about things and that's what I think makes a good teacher. (Grade 5)

A good teacher is someone who is pretty young so they know how the kid feels and to show power when it's needed, not when it's not. (Grade 6)

The last positive proposal is that *teachers should themselves obey the rules*. In their close attention to the 'fairness' of teachers, children are quick to spot and to pass judgment on teachers who do not themselves observe the rules. These comments come from all grade levels:

They don't let us eat in class. They say 'You're gonna drop crumbs on the floor' and *they* eat in class. (Grade 6)

I wish we could have a kind teacher who doesn't smoke in class and chew chewing gum in front of the class. (Grade 5)

She smells. She's always smoking. (Grade 2)

Smoking—it is a health hazard and could learn bad habits to the pupils. (Grade 5)

They don't use their manners enough. Like if you were to go and get him something from the office like a glass of water, which he is really fussy about it. He can't go and get it himself so he has to get Tracey. And he says, 'Tracey, go and get me a glass of water'. And he doesn't say 'please' or anything, and when she comes back he doesn't say 'thank you' or anything. (Grade 5)

In the children's eyes, 'do as I say', if not accompanied by 'do as I do', does not make a good teacher.

A little fantasy

We have so far dealt with working things out in terms of coming up with explanations and proposals for reform. Another way to cope with an imperfect situation is to resort to fantasy, sometimes combining it with a little humour. The fantasy may take the form of wishing for a change in the disposition of teachers:

> I would like to change teachers and make them friends with us kids. (Grade 5)
>
> I wish we could change the attitude of teachers and stop them hitting their pupils. (Grade 4)
>
> I wish we could change the teachers that push you around into kind teachers. (Grade 3)

More fancifully, one may think of ways in which teachers would simply not be present:

> I wish all the teachers were away. (Grade 3)
>
> I wish the teachers would be sacked and we have a robot who could walk and talk and give us no homework. (Grade 6)
>
> I wish I could change all the teachers into computers. (Grade 6)

Ideally, the disappearance would be at the child's command, with teachers in the position of being 'genies' who can be ordered to become invisible and to return to their bottle prisons:

> I wish our teacher would just disappear when we wanted her to, and be nice to us. (Grade 6)
>
> I wish that when the teacher said something awful—she would freeze. (Grade 4)
>
> I wish we had a plug-out teacher, that when he does his 'nana', we can pull the plug out. (Grade 5)

Fantasy concerning teachers may also take the form of a wish for power and revenge:

> I wish we could get our own back on teachers. (Grade 4)
>
> I wish I could break the cane into little pieces. (Grade 5)
>
> I wish I could change Mrs W. and her complaints, and shove a sock down her neck. (Grade 6)
>
> I'd change mean teachers into a piece of chicken on the table. (Grade 2)

The reversal of power could result from reversing roles, with the child becoming the teacher:

> I would like to teach the teacher a lesson because she gets the grumps with everyone. And she wouldn't like it if we get the grumps with her when she was naughty and we sent her out of the room up to Mrs D. (Grade 3)
>
> I would like to teach a teacher and show them how. And I would get cranky. Show them how we feel. (Grade 3)
>
> I would give them hard work like they give to us and show them what it feels like to be a kid. (Grade 3)
>
> We should teach the teachers what to do...Manners. I'd crack up on them and see how they like it. (Grade 6)

Individual differences

As in previous chapters, we wish to look at differences in the way the children work things out and in what they feel most strongly about—this time, with regard to their teachers.

Ways of working things out

We have noted a number of variations in the way children develop rules for teachers, explanations for teachers' behaviour, and proposals for change. Some children are clearly more for-giving of teachers than others, more willing to accept that teachers' actions are either for the good of children or stem from some reason other than sheer 'meanness'. Some are also more willing than others to accept the argument that difficulties in learning are their own problem, rather than the teacher's.

The form of individual difference we now wish to draw attention to has to do with the way children express a complaint or an argument for change and reform.

One aspect is the extent to which children express an argument in terms of themselves or others. Take comments on unfairness. Even in the senior grades, some children complain about unfairness in personal terms:

> I wish the teachers would be fair. Sometimes they let him go, but not me. (Grade 5)

> They are good when they give everyone a fair go. You want to go and ask them a question and they say, 'Wait on a minute'. And then they answer someone else. They get there before you. (Grade 6)

> Like another guy mucks up. And he [the teacher] screams a lot. And then I just lean over, and he screams at me. (Grade 5)

In contrast, others phrase their comments in terms of the way other children are treated:

> Some people get picked on...A girl in our class in craft, she was sitting in the corner this morning and she [the teacher] was picking on her a lot and she said 'Do you like sitting in the corner?'...And she didn't do anything to me. (Grade 5)

> There is a boy in our class, and everybody calls him 'Cry-baby', and he jumps out of the window. And it is not very funny, and it is not very fair, and I feel sad for him. (Grade 5)

In a way that moves even further away from talking about oneself, children may also comment on the way whole groups of children are treated:

> I don't like teachers when they pick sides with the girls or the boys. They treat the boys like they are angels and they treat the girls like they are nothing. (Grade 6)

> If you get sent to the office, I don't like it if the boy gets the strap and the girl doesn't. (Grade 6)

> I wish there were no teachers. Wish all the children were treated fairly. (Grade 6)

> I think a good teacher is a teacher with personality and she doesn't have a favourite and doesn't have a teacher's pet. Because sometimes, they usually don't like you and you don't try as hard. I think they should treat everyone the same. (Grade 6)

In many ways, age brings with it the use of more general and abstract statements. In the senior grades some children seem to have acquired—to a greater extent than others—the idea that it is important to phrase a complaint in a particular way. Some have certainly learned earlier than others that complaints about unfair treatments to others have less of a self-concerned air, and may be responded to more as matters of 'fact' than will statements about oneself.

Another view expressed in some children's comments—the desire for equity—reflects this more objective approach:[2]

> In our class we have got three groups. And there is one that are fairly good at some subjects, and some that are borderline, and the ones that aren't too good. And I like how our teacher explains to everybody. (Grade 6)

> I think a good teacher, he should spend more time with his class. And if there's one kid with a problem, he should go and help that child. And if someone else has got a problem at the same time, he could pick a smart person to go and help them while he's helping some other person. So everyone gets about the same amount of teacher. (Grade 6)

> I reckon a teacher should help the people who are not as good as the good ones. More than they do about the good ones. (Grade 6)

> They should be humourous. And they shouldn't expect too much out of the kids. Because if they aren't as good as other students, they should be helped more. (Grade 6)

> They should give more attention to the kids that can't do their work as well. (Grade 6)

Here we find, at this one grade level, statements about both principles of equality and equity (as well as the less sophisticated arguments that something is 'just not fair'). Age or grade level is undoubtedly a major factor in the extent to which principle is applied to situations.

The concern with fairness

As they grow older, children display an increasing concern with fairness and with rules. This seems to be a universal phenomenon[3]. Why the change occurs with age is a matter for debate. It may be that older children are more capable of taking the more general perspective involved in discussions about rules, or that older children draw upon a different set of experiences: they have been in several classrooms—or several schools—and have learned that things may be done in more than one way. Older children are also treated differently. They may move from a relatively permissive atmosphere in the junior grades of school to a more restrictive and discipline-oriented world.

We cannot settle the question of whether age differences represent shifts in capacity, experience, treatment, or some mixture of all of these. What the children bring to our attention, however, is the undeniable fact that some schools and classrooms provoke far more concern with fairness than do others. To bring out that point, we shall quote some of the extended discussions which took place. These bring out the significance of particular encounters with particular teachers in the development of a concern with fairness. In the two schools concerned, the interviewer has added some probing questions to those set as standard for all discussion groups. In both discussions, the interviewer is indicated by the letter 'I' and a child by the letter 'C'.

The first school is a coeducational state school in a small to middle-sized country town. The group consists of eight children from Grade 5, and the interviewer has made an effort to draw comment from each child.

I: Is there anything you don't like about school?

C: The teacher, because she drives you up the wall.

I: Why?

C: Oh, she tells you off *for nothing*. And another thing I don't like is maths, spelling, and reading.

I: What kind of things would you like a teacher to be like?

C: A kind teacher.

C: Just the teacher. When Mr Y. gets angry I think he's going to give me the cane. And he's always shouting.

I: Do you think he has a reason to shout?

C: Sometimes he might.

C: There are a lot of things I don't like about school. One, the teacher. He 'yabbas' on all day. And another thing. He always picks on us. And another thing I don't like about the teacher ...like you put up your hand and maybe he's doing paper work [and] he doesn't see your hand go up. But when you're just sitting there in school all day with your hand up and then he finally turns around and looks at you and then he says, 'Yes, Joan'. And then you ask him a question and then he shouts at you. And there's another thing I don't like about him. He said that if you ever want any help, well you should put up your hand and ask the teacher. And one day I put up my hand and asked the teacher—but he just said 'Oh, you never listen, do you?'

C: Well, the things I don't like at school is the teachers. Well, the the men teachers. I like the girl teachers better. Well, most times if you put up your hand to ask him something if you get stuck on a sum or something, and when he goes 'Yes?', he ends up blowing you up and says 'You didn't listen'.

C: The teachers are all right. He doesn't hardly go mad on me.

I: You think school is okay?

C: Yes.

I: Why is that?

C: He just understands me. Because when I was in Grade 4 and 5, he just told me how to do things.

I: Helps you out?

C: Yes.

C: I don't like Mr Y. he tells you, 'Fold your arms' and when you're folding your arms he says I'm dreaming and I'm not dreaming. Well, maths I don't really like. It's the hardest. Divide, he just gives you hard divide sums. And mostly English, 'cause you're writing all day and your hand gets tired.

C: I don't like the teachers. He goes nuts with you. He just keeps on blabbering till three o'clock and you do no art.

C: I don't really like teachers, especially Mr Y. Because we might be doing something wrong and it's this other kid's fault and he blows you up.

The second discussion group consists of children from Grade 3. The school in this case is in the outer suburbs of a large city. It is again a coeducational state school, but this one is classed as 'disadvantaged'. For the children, however, the significant features are again concerned with the behaviour of individual teachers towards individual children. After a discussion of what is liked about school (with an emphasis on sport and on 'hard' work with recognition), the interviewer asks: 'Is there anything you don't like about school?' The discussion soon settles on the way the headmaster (Mr M.) often 'gets mad':

I: What sort of things made him angry?

C: I don't know. Sometimes he is in a bad mood. And sometimes people have been naughty and things like that.

C: When Mr M. is angry, it is sometimes when people come into the school and they wreck the school. By breaking the awning and smashing windows, trying to set the school alight and all that.

I: Does that happen often?

C: Just about every weekend, after school. They tried to set a tree alight. Because most of the people, they don't like Mr M. They mainly like Mr H. He used to be a good teacher.

C: I agree with that. I like Mr H. better than Mr M., because Mr M. gets too involved. Like he always brings the police in, and people have been in trouble. And everything mainly happens because they don't like Mr M. Like some people write something on the wall.

C: I hate Mr M. too, because he says he likes animals. And he just sends David down to whack the dog.

C: I've got something to add to that. Mr M. had a favourite animal and his name is Grover. And he likes him and gives him food and everything and when another dog comes in he gives it the cane or something. And I don't think that's very fair.

C: If he does that to another dog, he should do it to Grover.

C: I'd ring the pound and get Grover to the pound.

C: One day Grover came and he got food. And then this other dog saw Grover getting food and the other dog came up, which was a boxer. And he sent David down and he got the cane and whacked him on the backside about three times. And I said to all my friends, 'The dog should have turned around and bit David and Mr M.'

I: This thing about unfair treatment. Does it happen to the children as well as to the dogs?

With this question, the floodgates are opened again for a discussion of fair and unfair treatment, once more ranging from general principles to very specific instances:

C: Yes, it does. When children are naughty, they get the cane or they are put on detention. But sometimes they get whacked by the ruler by the teachers.

I: What do you think should happen?

C: Some children deserve the cane and some don't. Some just get blamed for something they didn't do.

C; I think they should just get punished for a few days instead of getting the cane. Like Miranda said, they get it for no good reason.

C: In our class, his name is Larry. And he comes from New Zealand. And it is not fair. Because when we do maths, he just gets on with this little book and he just does stuff like 9 plus 3 and 4 plus 10. That's when we're doing fractions, multiplications and that, and division. And this is the first time he's done our work. And he's ten. And we say, if he doesn't pass in the exam, he doesn't have to repeat. Because he gets a chance. He goes back to New Zealand. That's not pretty fair, because he gets a chance. He goes back to New Zealand.

C: Like if he failed, and if he would've stayed here, he would probably repeat. But he is going back to New Zealand and he doesn't repeat.

C: He should be in Mr F.'s class.

I: That's a lower class?

C: Yes. He should be in a lower class because he doesn't know much of the things that we learn. And see, if he goes into Mr F.'s class, he starts learning.

I: It would have been easier for him. So really you're not saying it's his fault. He can't help it.

C: That's what we say. Sometimes we can't ... We don't know some of the work. It's not our fault. It's the teachers' fault because they don't teach us that work. And at the end of the year, they give us work that we haven't ever seen before.

C: My mother says that sometimes they give us work that we haven't ever seen before. And my mum doesn't like it sometimes. 'Cause like in the maths test, I haven't seen some of that work before and I don't think it's really fair.

I: Is there a lot on your test with things you haven't seen?

C: Not very much. But sometimes they are very hard things. And some people—like Miranda, she is a mathematician so she can do it—and we can't do it very good 'cause we haven't seen it. I don't think it's very fair sometimes.

Those Grade 3 children have an especially long list of 'unfairs' and a variety of examples. We have quoted from them at length partly to indicate the way some schools seem to be more pre-occupied with fairness than are others. The discussion also helps us illustrate some important aspects of children's discussions.

The first is the everyday quality of comments on teachers. Even if some of the recital is helped by the interviewer's questions, a great deal of it is part of the children's general conversations ('and we say ...'), given further legitimacy by one's parents ('My mother says ...').

The second has to do with the variety of events that get drawn into the absorbing topic of fairness. The third has to do with what children regard as significant. The incident of Mr M. and his dog is clearly of more interest to the children than Mr M.'s act of calling in the police. The dog is *real* proof of Mr M.'s unfairness. Finally, these discussions illustrate a process of learning. it is important to be able to add something to the conversation ('I've got something to add to that ...'). This must be something that will be accepted by the group as interesting, even if exaggeration is added to the legitimate grievance ('And when you're just sitting there in school all day with your hand up').

We know from studies in several countries that children in the upper grades of primary school are deeply interested in the topic of fairness. What individual teachers do is to add fuel to a fire that seems ready to burn, convincing some children, more so than others, that school is indeed often far from fair.

4
LIFE AT SCHOOL:
activities

Just as we looked at the activities associated with the home setting in Chapter 2, now we turn our attention to activities in the school setting—again with the recognition that people and activities are inter-related.

We start by asking: What are some of the general features of school activities? Do they differ greatly from activities at home? What effect do these features have on the way children perceive school activities and the way they feel about them?

To start with, school is mainly about 'learning'. Most of the learning, however, is concerned with things that are not present. Most of the activities that take place at home in the morning are in context; most are also immediately comprehensible—that is, there is a clear reason for eating breakfast or getting dressed. In contrast, much of the learning that takes place in school is *learning out of context*. This feature of school has been commented on with particular clarity by Bruner.[1] There are times, he points out, when we learn 'on the job': we learn to cook, for instance, in the kitchen and by actually cooking. More often, in any modern society, learning is 'off the job'. We sit in a classroom; we read about things that others have done or that we might do; we see pictures of people and animals no longer able to be seen even if we move out of the classroom. Small wonder that a second-grader says wistfully: 'I wish there were still dinosaurs on earth'.

This feature of school, we shall see, often means a struggle to make connections between the world of school and the 'real' world and, at times, a sense of dissatisfaction with what school learning covers, especially in comparison with all the interesting topics it could cover.

School learning is also a constantly changing scene. We noted in Chapter 3 that teachers change. To an even greater extent, activities also change. The essence of school learning, in fact, is that you constantly encounter changes and transitions. You may at home master household tasks and establish a comfortable routine for the start or end of the day. In the context of household tasks, it is rarely suggested that the mastery of one activity will be the usual signal for change to another. But constant movement is the essence of school learning: its potential challenge and reward, its potential insecurity and misery.

Novel situations, we have proposed, call for particular attention to the expectations people bring with them. Children do not come empty-minded to first grade or to any new grade in school. Moreover, their expectations colour the way they feel about school and the way in which they think about methods of improving the situation. That point was made in Chapter 3 with regard to teachers. It applies also to the activities of school. In many ways, children facing school activities remind us of people disappointed with a restaurant. They often find the bill of fare rather narrow in its range or, regarding the things they like, rather skimpy in amount. They may also find the price higher than expected, in the sense of having to put up with aspects that are 'boring' or 'too hard'.

Can we be more specific about children's expectations with regard to school activities? We shall be dealing with four pervasive hopes: you will learn 'everything'; you will learn 'useful' things; you will like the work; and the day will not be 'all work'.

These expectations underlie the features children like and dislike about school, and their proposals for change in both the timing of activities and the content of the curriculum. When their expectations are met, children regard school as a fine place. When they are not, dissatisfaction and proposals for change abound.

We will look at each of these expectations and at the children's proposals for change. In doing so, we shall be using answers from several questions. Children were asked: 'What do you like about school?'; 'What don't you like about school?'; 'Is there anything you would like to learn more of at school?'; 'What makes a good teacher?'. These questions were discussed in groups, with each child prompted to make a comment. For a final question—'If you could change one thing about school, what would that be?'—each child wrote out an answer.

First we will present some of the frequency counts for the two questions concerning wishes for change, and liked and disliked features of school. These frequency counts indicate the relative prominence of various issues. We shall start by seeing how we can group the *wishes for change*. Once we eliminated answers that were irrelevant to school, there were 824 codable wishes for juniors, and 1412 for seniors. To avoid the figures being over-influenced by those children who offered many wishes, we present frequency counts for just the first wish expressed by a child (753 juniors, 954 seniors). The results are in fact much the same as when all wishes are included.

Figure 4.1 shows how the first wishes were distributed. It brings out first of all the importance of two factors that were prominent in the wishes for changes in morning routines at home (Chapter 2): namely, time and choice.

Time, for instance, is the subject of a desired area of change

Juniors   **Seniors**

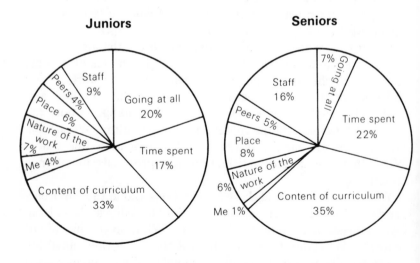

Figure 4.1 Children's wishes for changes in school, expressed as percentages of all wishes for change.

expressed by both juniors and seniors (17 per cent of juniors' wishes, 22 per cent of seniors'). The wishes about time in relation to school turn out to be primarily of three kinds: wishes for less time at school (53 per cent and 62 per cent, respectively, of juniors' and seniors' wishes concerning time), for a reorganisation of the timetable (25 per cent and 28 per cent), and for a careful separation of 'work time' from 'free time' (22 per cent and 10 per cent), a wish that covers both references to homework and to teachers cutting into recess or lunchtime with classroom activities.

The factor of choice appears this time in the form of wishes for a change in the content of the curriculum (33 per cent of juniors, 35 per cent of seniors): more of some topics and less of others. The wishes are mainly in the form of wishes for 'more'. When we break them down, we find that wishes for more sport, games, and playing lead the list (34 per cent of juniors' wishes for more of a certain activity, 37 per cent of seniors). The next highest on the list are wishes for more of the subjects often termed 'extras' (art, craft, and to a lesser extent, music and religion). These account for 24 per cent and 18 per cent of the wishes for change in the school curriculum. In contrast, 'standard' school subjects account for 9 per cent of both juniors' and seniors' desires for change in this area. However, where the juniors often wish for more 'hard work' and more 'tests' (20 per cent), the seniors do so only rarely (5 per cent). The seniors suggest more often that there be more interest and variety (4 per cent for juniors, 12 per cent for seniors), and that there be more 'useful' topics (6 per cent for juniors, 13 per cent for seniors).

Another type of desire for change has to do with school as a place, mainly in the form of wishes to spend more time 'outside'. Then there were those comments concerned with the nature of the work: work that is 'boring', 'too hard', or accompanied by tests you dislike. A third has to do with people: the peers you sit with, play with, or work with and the staff (teachers) who turn out to be neither as friendly nor as helpful as one might wish.

Are there major differences between juniors and seniors? One concerns the wish not to go to school at all, to stay at home and do something else. This simply-expressed wish is frequent among the juniors (20 per cent) but occurs less often among the seniors (7 per cent). The seniors (Grades 4, 5 and 6) seem to have settled in. The other noticeable difference has to do with the frequency with which the desire for change is focussed on teachers, being more pronounced among seniors (16 per cent) than among the juniors (9 per cent).

Liked and disliked features of school. Questions about what children liked and disliked yielded a wide variety of answers. Table 4.1 gives the percentages, indicating the extent to which particular features stand out in children's perspectives. We may summarise these by saying that: sport and games, and the 'extra' subjects, are liked by many and disliked by few; standard school subjects are also liked by many (although among the juniors, an equal number dislike them, and among the seniors, the number of dislikes is in fact larger than the number of likes); and teachers are mentioned mainly in the 'disliked' comments by seniors.

Table 4.1   The most frequent comments concerning activities and people, among the aspects of school mentioned as liked or disliked.

	Juniors'		Seniors'	
	Positive	Negative	Positive	Negative
Sport, games, playing	32	3	33	4
'Extra' subjects				
(e.g. art, craft, music)	15	1	20	3
Standard subjects	43	45	30	48
Peers	3	8	7	2
Teachers	2	12	3	24
Miscellaneous	5	31	7	19

Why do children like some subjects rather than others? The appeal of sport, games and playing may seem fairly apparent. But why do the standard school subjects receive such mixed reviews? Our first thought was that some particular school subjects might be higher on the 'like' or 'dislike' lists than others. We even yielded to the temptation of counting how often maths, in any of its forms, appeared on the 'liked' and 'disliked' lists. It appeared equally often on each. That result may be reassuring to teachers. It left us no further forward, however, in understanding the bases for likes and dislikes.

The underlying basis to likes, dislikes, and wishes for change—we came to feel—lay in the way that children's experiences matched the hopes and expectations they brought to school and in their ideas about how one learns. With the basic frequency counts as one guide, and with the children's own words as another, we drew out the four large hopes and expectations to which we now turn.

Hopes, expectations, and reality

To new settings, we have argued, we bring hopes and expectations about what we shall encounter, about what both the work and the play will be like. The outcome may be one of pleasant surprise, disappointment, or a solid sense of satisfaction that what had been expected was in fact found. Expectations colour the perceptions of what one finds and the feelings to which this gives rise. Children coming into school or into a new grade are no exception. Their expectations affect their perspectives on school activities and on the way these are managed by teachers. We review four pervasive expectations and some of their consequences.

You will learn everything

Children bring to the activities of school an enormous and varied appetite. Particularly at the outset, they want 'to know everything', as one second-grader put it. They want:

To learn how to spell great big words. (Grade 1)

To stay at school all night and write more stories. (Grade 2)

To learn more about aeroplanes and radio control and more about tying up shoelaces and more about maths. (Grade 3)

To learn more things every day. (Grade 4)

To see things you have never seen before. (Grade 5)

To learn more about God and blind people and animals and making things. (Grade 5)

What does 'learning everything' involve? The children's comments bring out for us two forms of learning: *learning about and learning how*[2].

Suppose we take the topics mentioned by juniors when asked what they wish to 'learn more of'. Some of these wishes are for information, for facts 'about'. These cover the wish to learn about 'how newspapers are made', 'how a baby comes out of a tummy', 'how they make horseshoes', 'how they make ice-cream', or 'how animals sometimes understand us'. Other wishes are for skill, for learning 'how to': 'how to tell the time', 'how to separate honey', 'how to work out money when you go in the shop', 'how to do magic', 'how to set the alarm clock', 'how to stand on my head', 'how to make pies', 'how to ride a bike and not crash into people'.

Does a distinction between knowing about and knowing how matter? The children's comments bring out three ways in which it does. First, 'how to' requires a formula. Second, you may not be able to find the formula yourself, making you particularly dependent upon others to 'explain' or 'show you how'.

Third, some school subjects seem to fall more than others do into the 'how to' category. One may learn *about* cavemen, the stars, history, or how the heart works. But you have to know *how* to spell, write a poem or an essay, read, do long division or fractions. Within these 'how to' content areas, there may be as well some where you are particularly dependent on someone else supplying the formula: that is, you see yourself as less likely to discover 'how to' by yourself. The extent to which mathematics is greeted with joy or dismay may reflect the extent to which it contains these features:

> I don't like maths. I can't do it half the time. (Grade 5)
>
> I don't like it when we have maths and I get in a fuss about it because I can't do it. (Grade 6)
>
> I get mad when I cannot do the maths. (Grade 4)
>
> I'm not very good at mathematics and I'd like to learn more about maths. I couldn't do a divide sum a little short way. I just couldn't do it that way. And ever since I learned this other new way, I can do it quick as a flash. (Grade 5)
>
> If she is kind and if you get a sum wrong or something and if you got twenty sums and you got half of them wrong or all of them wrong, and she would just sit down and explain. Not like Mrs W. She will say, 'I told you how to do it'. (Grade 4)

Finally, as the last comment implies, the *evaluation of teachers* is related to the extent to which they provide the magic formulae that tell you 'how to' and that work well:

> A good teacher teaches you how. (Grade 6)

I don't like it when they teach you phonetics and you get a word like that and you write it down and you get it wrong. (Grade 5)

I think Miss S. is good because she tells you about it. She tells you a lot of ways to do it. (Grade 5)

I like a teacher who explains what you do when you are wrong. Like they say, 'Try and keep space between things'. (Grade 5)

As that last comment suggests, the formulae provided may be quite simple. But they are specific and they can be immediately applied.

The reality. Children, naturally, do not 'learn everything' at school. They are neither provided with all the information they seek, nor with all the skills and formulae they wish for. We shall take up their proposals for additions to the curriculum in the section on working things out. For the moment, the sense of disappointment is well conveyed in a blistering comment by a fifth-grader, from a school in a mining area:

CHILD: It is all the same thing every day—*same subjects*. All she has given us for weeks is things about ancient cavemen and you get sick and tired of it, and you do about 16 pages in those big project books, and it is real boring. She will keep on going and keep us in, and all the other classes are early or are out on time and we are the last to get out.

INTERVIEWER: Would you like to be asked what type of social studies you would like to do?

CHILD: Yes.

INTERVIEWER: What kind of social studies would you say?

CHILD: I think we should just get outside the classroom and just explore the air and run around and that. History.

INTERVIEWER: What kind of history?

CHILD: All of it. About the mines and all of the big things that work out there, like the big loaders and inside the mines. Anything but cavemen.

You will learn useful things

Going to school is a major and exciting transition in child's life. It is exciting in part because it is felt to be irrevocable. One cannot go back to being a 'pre-schooler'. It is also exciting because it is seen as an indispensable access route to new forms of skill and to becoming 'grown-up'. Not to go to school, some children tell us, is to be a 'baby', a state wistfully referred to by a first-grader:

> I wish I was a baby still. I wish I was not at school because I hate school very much.

Not to go to school is also to run the risk of being unemployed and, far more often mentioned, the risk of growing up 'dumb'.

> You learn a lot. And if you didn't learn, when you grew up, you wouldn't know anything. (Grade 2)
>
> If you don't have more exams, you don't grow up. (Grade 3)
> ... if you don't learn about it [other countries] at school, you won't learn about it. (Grade 5)

This sense of school as the *only* place where you learn comes through also in the lack of comment about any alternative to school. An occasional child sees the possibility of some deferment. In the words of a fourth-grader:

> I don't really want to learn more, because we are only young; and I would like to keep all the harder parts until we are at high school.

In all the comments throughout the country, however, there was only one explicit mention that there might be an alternative to school—namely 'travel'.

Can we be more precise about what children see as useful? The usefulness most often mentioned is for future participation in the paid work force:

> More about working like mummy because she gets money for working. (Grade 1)
>
> I'd like to learn more about what it's like when you get older: how to get a job and what it's like and everything. (Grade 4)
>
> More about trucks, because I want to be a good truckie and be interstate. (Grade 5)

The reality. A striking feature of the children's comments is a general vagueness about usefulness. In some cases, the value of school learning is seen only in very general terms. For example:

> I don't mind the work if it helps me in the future. (Grade 6)

More often, the children offer some indication of how they see a link between their present learning and the needs of the future. These links, however, are still—to the adult eye—very vague. We have gone through all the future-oriented reasons spontaneously given for wishing to alter the school curriculum or to learn more about a particular topic, asking: What connections between present and future do these children see?

One form is the argument that 'earlier is better', apparently accepted at a young age. For example:

> They could make little cars so that you could learn for children. When you grow up, you have a bigger car, so you know how to drive and you don't have to learn it. (Grade 4)

> The teachers could teach the girls to cook. When they grow up they can cook. (Grade 5)

> I'd like to have another cooking day like last year. Because when you grow up and when you leave school that can also help you when you grow up. And I wouldn't like to go out every night and buy my own meal. That would be too dear. (Grade 5)

That same type of argument underlies the proposal that one should study in school the occupation one wishes to follow in later life:

> I'd like to learn more about doctors, because when I grow up I'd like to be a doctor. (Grade 4)

> How to work like a policeman, because I want to grow up to be one. (Grade 1)

> Like how to do what you want. Like people might want to be a vet when they grow up and they study what they want to be when they grow up. (Grade 5)

Children also offer attempts to put together specific school topics with the requirements of future jobs. Sometimes, the emphasis is only on the school topics:

> More maths because when you are older you mainly have to do things that are involved in maths. (Grade 6)

> More art and maths because you mainly need these two subjects and spelling later in life. (Grade 5)

> More about science and social studies because it helps you get jobs. (Grade 5)

Some children, however, do specify a more definite link. 'More sums, because I'm going to be a bank man when I grow up', says a first-grader. With this kind of forward perception, you need 'spelling to be a teacher', and 'to know about dogs' to be a vet, trucks to be a truck driver, mines to be a miner, cars to be a mechanic. On this basis, a special part of the curriculum may even be perceived as undesirable:

> If anything would be changed, it would be sport. You don't need to know about sports if you are going to be an office lady. (Grade 5)

We quote these comments as a way of underlining, not the children's incompetence, but the nature of a great deal of school learning. On the one hand is the children's wish for useful and 'real' knowledge. On the other is the fact that school usually deals with objects and events at a distance: with cavemen and dinosaurs no longer present on earth, with jobs often known about only by name, with places known only as coloured areas on maps. Small wonder that so many of the proposals for curriculum change are in the direction of knowledge that is more closely tied to the real world.

You will like the work

Children often come to school with a readiness to work and an interest in having 'lots to do'. For example:

> Wish we would have enough work to keep us going all day. (Grade 5)
>
> I don't like wasting time, just mucking around. (Grade 5)

They also often come with an interest in skill and in the proofs of skill. The signs that they are becoming 'good at things' may lie in the capacity to do 'hard work' or in their teacher's recognition. Feelings in this area are more openly expressed by the juniors, but are present also in the senior grades:

> I wish for more hard work. (Grade 1)
>
> I wish for more reading, so I can learn to read hard work. (Grade 2)
>
> I like it when they mark you work and tell you it's good. (Grade 1)
>
> I like Mrs C. because she gives you pretty hard work and after that she gives you pretty lots of games. (Grade 2)
>
> When you be good, they be good to you and all that, and they give you stars and all that, stars in your book, and they write in your book 'Good work'. (Grade 3)
>
> I like the times table and hard work. (Grade 2)

The work is too easy. (Grade 2)

Wish we could get more and much harder work. (Grade 5)

We don't get enough hard words. They should be harder.
(Grade 5)

The strength of this early interest in work and in the proofs of skill is indicated by the fact that a wish for more hard work and more tests accounts for 20 per cent of the juniors' wishes for change in the curriculum, although it accounts for only 5 per cent of the seniors' nominations for change.

The reality. What happens to this great interest in being challenged, in coping with hard, interesting work?

For one thing, the work sometimes turns out to be '*too hard*': a comment that needs some unravelling. It sometimes refers to the fact that the work is exhausting. 'I don't like maths because it strains your brain', says a fourth-grader. More often, the negative side emerges when the work can't be coped with:

I hate it when you have to do something and you can't figure it out. (Grade 3)

I don't like it when we get a big stack of work and we don't know how to do it. (Grade 4)

Written expression. That's hard. Because you can't think of anything to write. I can't think of words and all that and where you put full stops and commas and that. (Grade 5)

I don't like number tests, because I get them all wrong. (Grade 2)

I don't like it at school because when you have a test and you can't do it, you feel all upset and you think: 'What is going to happen to me?'. (Grade 5)

I don't mind tests if you know how to do them. But I wish the teacher wouldn't yell all the marks and everyone looks at you. (Grade 5)

Once again, the children's expectations and encounters with reality colour the perception of teachers and the liking and disliking of subjects. The 'good' teacher, we are told, walks a fine line between work that is hard enough to be challenging, which gives you a good feeling when you manage it, and work that is so hard you are exhausted or can't cope:

She gives you hard work and that. She's a good teacher because it makes you think. (Grade 3)

A good teacher is someone who doesn't set you work at an easy level. They let you work at a harder level. (Grade 5)

They teach you easy first and then they work up to harder things so you can do them. (Grade 5)

A good teacher teaches you how to do things properly and then they're not too hard. (Grade 6)

What about the perception of particular school subjects? It is—to put the matter simply—difficult to like subjects you are not good at. The point is made with reference to a variety of school subjects:

I like spelling. I am a good speller. (Grade 2)

I hate spelling. I usually get bad marks. (Grade 5)

I don't like English and maths. They are my worst subjects. (Grade 3)

I don't like music because I'm not that good at it. (Grade 6)

I don't like sport because I'm not a good runner. (Grade 6)

It may be possible to like a subject you are not good at. That mainly occurs, we suspect, when you think you are likely to improve.

Subjects that are 'too hard' represent one form of disappointment, one way in which children find that school does not meet their need for work they will like and can cope with. The second avenue to disappointment is that the work is often '*boring*'.

'Boring' is an often-used word, with several meanings. It means first of all having nothing to do:

I wish I could work all the time, because I get bored sometimes. (Grade 1)

I like school because there's plenty of things to do. At home you get bored all day. (Grade 4)

It also means not doing the same thing all the time:

I don't like spelling and reading, because it's boring and you have to learn it lots of times. You have to read the page over and over and I get sick of it. (Grade 2)

You write and then you make a mistake and write it again and you keep on writing it until you get it right. (Grade 3)

We do something one day. Then we do the same thing the next day, and nearly all through the week sometimes. (Grade 5)

I don't like maths, because you do it every day and you get sick of it if you do it every day. (Grade 6)

Finally, 'boring' means that the activity is dull, that there is a lack of liveliness to the way things are taught, and an absence of 'fun':

I wish for fun with our lesson but still work hard. (Grade 4)

More time to work in groups and making our activities more fun. For instance, if we're studying clothes, have a fashion show. (Grade 6)

'Boring' is not the only word that needs untangling. All told, three words are mentioned in this type of discussion: 'work', 'play', and 'fun'. 'Work' and 'play' appear to be used as opposites. 'Work' and 'fun' are seen by the children as not necessarily opposite, even though some teachers appear to be suspected of seeing the two as incompatible. Consider:

I wish we could have more time for fun, and more interesting subjects so some work would seem like fun. (Grade 6)

I wish we could do things in a fun way rather than straight out work. (Grade 5)

We could play Bingo at maths times. Then the teachers can't complain about us doing no work because Bingo, that's a maths game. (Grade 5)

Once again, disappointment—in the form of feelings about monotony and variety—affects the way learning and teachers are perceived. Witness the comments:

The thing I don't like about school is when you're ready to learn something and the teacher does it over and over again and you get lazy and she starts screaming at you. (Grade 6)

A good teacher doesn't plug on about the same thing all the time. (Grade 5)

A good teacher reads stories in between subjects, not giving you subject after subject after subject. (Grade 6)

The day will not be all work

We have just noted that the children distinguish three forms of activity ('work', 'play' and 'fun'), and hope that school will contain some of each type of activity.

This hope is underlined by the importance children give, when asked what they like about school, to the activities of sport, games, and 'just playing' (Table 4.1). It is underlined still further by the frequency with which children wish for *more outside time*. Let me out! is their frequent cry.

The wishes for outside time especially remind us of what school is like as a place. School does contain some outdoor space and children sometimes go on excursions. Most of the time, however, the activities of learning are linked to a specific place: you are tied to a desk, a classroom.[3] Small wonder then that children often express a sense of confinement, and that one of the things they wish to change is the limiting of space and movement. The comments come from many grade levels:

I wish to play outside. (Grade 2)

Wish we could go outside to do work. (Grade 3)

Wish we could change our room now and then. (Grade 4)

Wish we could have classes outside under the trees when it's hot. (Grade 5)

We have never been outside. Like during classes, we have never been outside to play games and we have sport only on Fridays and that's all. (Grade 6)

We have said that hopes and expectations affect the way one feels about any new setting, and the way people in that setting are perceived. School as a place provides a prime example. The hope that one will not always be inside gives rise to great indignation when outside time is denied or cut back as a penalty. A fifth-grader expresses this with vehemence:

I don't like it when Sir says at the beginning of the year that he is going to take us on all these excursions to the Jenolan Caves and he was going to take us to the army barracks and camps and he doesn't do that ... they won't take you there because of a few silly people. And we say sometimes, 'Admit it' and we say, 'Why not leave the silly people behind and take the good people'. He said he was going to take us to an area tomorrow where big things are and they open up the dome ... and you look at the moon and that, and he said he is taking us on a school camp and he didn't do that. And we are having a farewell for Grade 6, and there are a lot of things we missed and he said we could probably do. And he said we could do it and now we can't do it. Someone won't let us do hardly any of it.

The reverse image of this villainous 'Sir' is the good teacher who opens up physical space. The good teacher takes you on picnics and excursions. The good teacher also gives you back some of your access to the outdoors. The comments come from juniors and seniors:

> Takes you outside to teach you. (Grade 2)
>
> Lets us go out just about every day. Even she let us go out at little lunch [recess] and big lunch, and even at home time and she let us go out and play games. (Grade 2)
>
> Takes you out to games a lot. (Grade 4)
>
> Lets us out of the classroom. (Grade 6)
>
> Takes you out for sport and doesn't keep you in. (Grade 4)
>
> Men teachers are better than lady teachers because they always make the children have sport every afternoon. (Grade 5)
>
> I reckon he was a good teacher: he was strict but he gave us sport. (Grade 5)

Perhaps confinement would be less of a problem if the inside space were more attractive. Overall, however, there are few comments about the aesthetics of classrooms. The most detailed comment comes from a fifth-grader who has seen that other arrangements are possible:

> I wish that our school had horses to ride, a pool to swim in, tennis courts, carpet in every room and the classrooms were decorated with art and projects. I have been to an American school. It is much better than ours. Even they have trampolines.

Most children, however, concentrate their gaze on being 'out' rather than on making being 'in' more attractive. It is a rare child who turns 'interior decorator', either realistically or in the exuberant approach of a third-grader wishing for '20 000 swings in the classroom'!

Working things out: time changes

In the school setting, the problems of time and the proposals for improvement do in fact repeat some of the themes noted for activities at home. That is not surprising, since school impinges on the home setting largely by way of setting the time frame for the morning. In addition, wishes about time in relation to school bring out some new proposals for reform or problem-solving. The three main proposals are for less time at school, reorganisation of the timetable, and a careful separation of 'school time' and 'our time'.

Less time at school

The wish for shorter hours takes the form of cutting down at all parts of the day. It is not simply the morning pressure that is being reflected:

> Wish we could start at 11.00, end at 1.00. (Grade 5)
>
> Wish we started at 10.00 and ended at 2.00. (Grade 4)
>
> Wish we did not have such a long day at school. (Grade 4)
>
> Wish we had computers to make the day go faster. (Grade 5)

Less time at school could also be accomplished by moving the days around or cutting down the total number of years spent at school. For example:

> Wish we could have the weekend at school and the rest of the week for a holiday. (Grade 4)
>
> Wish Wednesday was a holiday. (Grade 5)
>
> Wish we did not go so many years to school. (Grade 6)

Reorganise the timetable

A simple wish for shorter hours might be set aside as being largely a fantasy, however creative. Reorganising a timetable, however, is a more realistic goal. It is also an interesting version of the problem-solving we saw in relation to activities at the start of the day (Chapter 2), namely locating the moveable parts.

Why do children wish to reorganise the timetable in particular ways? With regard to home activities at the start of the day, a major source of desire for change was the wish for more sleep. In the school setting, the goals of reform are a little more complex. One goal is again the wish to *bring body time and clock time closer together*, expressed particularly clearly in a number of juniors' comments about what they do not like about school, but not exclusive to juniors:

You can't get a drink when you're thirsty. (Grade 1)

You can't go to the toilet when you want to. (Grade 1)

You can't put your head on your desk after lunch. (Grade 2)

When you were in kindergarten and you got tired, you could have a rest, but while you're in Grade 2, you're not allowed to have a rest. (Grade 2)

You can't read a book in the library if you're tired. (Grade 5)

You need a break. You're writing all day and your hand gets tired. (Grade 4)

One way to bring body time and clock time a little closer together is to arrange for 'breaks'. Another is to move school subjects from one time slot to another. For example:

Easy things right after lunch. (Grade 2)

I wish reading was in the morning instead of afternoon because everybody is hot and wants to do something else. (Grade 4)

A second goal is the *provision of choice*:

I wish I could work my own timetables. (Grade 5)

Wish we could choose the subjects we do *first*, instead of being told that something had to be done first, and then something else. (Grade 4)

Wish there was some time in the day when every child got to do something they like. (Grade 4)

A third goal in reform proposals is the wish to *match activity time to interest time*. What is objected to with special force is the arbitrary ending of an activity:

You're just getting really started on something and you want to keep going, and the teacher says, 'Right, now we're going to do something else'. Why can't we keep going till we're finished?. (Grade 6)

I feel upset because when you're just starting things you have to move on to something else. (Grade 4)

I don't like it when we stop a subject and go on with it the next day 'cause you might forget about it and how to do it and you just take up that time to figure it out again. (Grade 5)

We have then three problems with the school timetable: the lack of suitable links with time, the lack of choice as to when work is done, and the lack of match to interest time. In the children's eyes, all three problems could be coped with by moving activities from one time slot to another.

Keep 'school time' and 'our time' separate

Class time is for 'work'. Recess, lunch, and after school are not. The latter times are given a variety of names: 'free time', 'normal time', 'our time of rest', 'our time for other things'. The distinction colours discussions of homework and of being kept in, sometimes combined:

> You go to school and do work and then you go home and have to do homework there as well. (Grade 5)

> Homework, well, you're working all day at school and when you get home you should be able to play. (Grade 4)

> I don't like assignments 'cause when you go home your mother keeps nagging at you about getting it done and she won't let you watch telly or anything. (Grade 6)

> I don't like it when you are sick and you come back to school and you have to do the maths paper while the other kids are having free time. (Grade 3)

> I don't like it when you don't do your homework and they tell you to do it at little lunch [recess]. (Grade 6)

For children as well as adults, it seems, work is unpopular when it has to be 'taken home' or done in one's 'own time'. The solution, in the children's eyes, is simple: work in work time, and have it clearly separated from 'our time for other things'.

Working things out: curriculum changes

In the course of looking at children's hopes, expectations, and encounters with reality, we have been presented with a number of proposals for reform: more time outside; more choice of topic and timing; more interesting ways of teaching; more time spent showing you 'how', and more 'useful' knowledge.

We now wish to take up two widespread proposals for change. These become prominent when children are asked: 'Is there anything you'd like to learn more about?'. Table 4.2 gives the children's nominations.

It is reassuring to see a sizeable number of nominations given to

Table 4.2 Nominations for subjects and activities about which children wanted to learn more (shown as percentages of all nominations for changes in school)

	Juniors %	Seniors %
Sport, games, playing	19	19
'Extra' subjects (e.g. art, craft, music)	10	9
Standard subjects	20	18
Items not on the usual curriculum	51	54

the subjects we have called 'standard' (in the children's terms, these are subjects such as spelling, reading, writing, sums, fractions history, geography, social studies). These subjects account for 20 per cent of the juniors' and 18 per cent of the seniors' for 20 per cent of the juniors' and 18 per cent of the seniors' nominations: percentages higher than those for the subjects often called 'extras' (art, craft, music, religion, library), (10 per cent for increased time at outside activities: sport, games, playing (19 per cent for juniors and for seniors). The nominations for sport, games and playing, however, are high when one considers that the question—anything you'd like to *learn* more about—slants the answers somewhat away from these activities.

The largest set of nominations, however, is for a set of items that are not normally regarded as subjects or activities on the school curriculum, in contrast to the three other categories. These items cover topics ranging from animals, nature and rocks, to mines, babies, stars, newspapers, love, God, politics, and being an adult. They also cover learning how to do a multiplicity of things, from separating honey to playing the guitar, standing on one's head, or reading the T.V. guide. Such nominations account for 51 per cent of the juniors' wishes and 54 per cent of the seniors'.

To go a little below the surface of these nominated items, we shall look at two aspects. One is an unexpected grouping of two activities: sport and art. The other is the nature of the items not on the usual curriculum.

An unexpected grouping: sport and art

Whenever we attempt to exchange one activity for another—to move the parts around—it is useful to know what people regard as equivalent parts. Is time off in the morning, for example, accepted as equivalent to time worked after the usual hour of finishing work? Is extra time on one activity counted as compensating for less time on another? Without a knowledge of such equivalences, we may have difficulty in getting our proposals accepted, or in understanding the substitutions they propose.

For these reasons, we were intrigued to note that children often spoke of sport and art as equivalent. They often put these two subjects together, either in a single phrase ('sport and art') or in a sentence form that treats the two as equivalent:

> More art and sport. (Grade 4)
>
> Two periods of art and sport a week. (Grade 6)
>
> More sport in winter and craft in summer. (Grade 5)
>
> More P.E. and other activities like painting. (Grade 6)
>
> More art, craft, sport—no maths or English. (Grade 5)
>
> Gymnastics, and how to do macrame better. (Grade 5)
>
> More time for sports and crafts. (Grade 5)
>
> Instead of drawing, have P.E. (Grade 3)
>
> Cut down on art and craft and sport, and learn a few more languages like French, German, Latin and Egyptian. (Grade 6)

'Sport' for these children covers a variety of activities. So also does 'art' or 'craft' (for example, 'Wish I could stay in the art room all day and do woodwork'). What do all these activities have in common? They appear first of all to be outside the usual category of 'work':

> Half the day for sport and some art and some work. (Grade 3)
>
> More sport, less school work, more craft time. (Grade 5)
>
> More sport and more free time. We could learn more about pottery and art. (Grade 4)

'Sport and art' also seem to share a freedom of movement, a chance to have more choice in what you do, and a chance to exercise some skill. When those features disappear, even sport, art and craft may move on to the disliked list:

> I don't like sewing 'cause the teacher makes us make silly things. (Grade 6)
>
> There are not enough things to do in playtime and in craft. I don't

like that, because it is boring sometimes. I like making things.
That's my hobby. But some of the things we make are not very
good. (Grade 6)

I wish when we are having art, you can make what you want.
(Grade 3)

I used to like art but now we've got a teacher who takes up half our
time explaining things. (Grade 5)

Items not on the usual curriculum

On the list of what children wish to learn more about is a hefty
proportion of items not usually found on the school curriculum.
For some children, these 'outside' topics constitute their entire
list. A second-grader in a mining town provides an example:

... more about how rocks are made and mining; how gold is found
and about generators that have been working for years.

What does the children's diverse collection of interests cover?
Within it, there are two fairly large categories: firstly, nature and
animals, and secondly, other cultures and languages. Mentions of
'nature and animals' are especially marked among the juniors (14
per cent of all 'more-of' nominations by juniors; 8 per cent for
seniors). Mentions of other cultures and other languages rise from
7 per cent of all 'more-of' nominations among juniors to 16 per
cent among seniors.

We shall use these two categories to bring out the impressive
quality of children's interests, and some of the sources of their
interests. The references to animals, for instance, reflect the way
children observe the world around them, often starting with
apparently simple events, and then build their observations into
wide-ranging questions:

More about how the plant leaves open. (Grade 2)

How animals grow, how they catch their food, and how they move
their bodies. (Grade 2)

How animals survive. We have all the things and they don't have as
many. Like—they have half the things but they have to survive
harder than we do. (Grade 4)

The same attention to both detail and the larger questions
appears in comments on other places and other cultures:

The different children in the world: what they do and how they are
treated at school. (Grade 2)

More about space, because I've always wondered what it would be
like up there on the moon. (Grade 5)

What other countries are like—like China. Lots of people in China
eat rice and we eat fish and chips. (Grade 2)

How they thought of the names of countries and how they built the
countries and how some people don't speak the same as us.
(Grade 5)

Learning about other people in other countries and how they
survive the hot summer and the cold winter in other places
(Grade 6)

Most of these recommendations stem from children's observa-
tion of the world around them. We have ended with great respect
for the liveliness with which children survey their world, and with
the hope that school can either meet their interests or leave intact
their sense of wonder. In comparison with the world that can be
observed, school contains a massive amount of material on events
that have passed and beings that can no longer be seen. The
chidren are proposing a shift in the balance of curriculum topics
so that more comes from the 'real' world.

Individual differences

We have outlined, in previous chapters, two areas in which
individuals may differ in their daily lives: in the issues they
consider to be important and in the way that these issues are
worked out or thought about. The transition to school brings out
new forms of those differences.

The burning issues

Not every child is equally concerned with the nature of learning,
the limitations of the school curriculum, or with the need for
change. There are, in fact, a few who wish for little or no change:

I wish for everything to stay the same please, because I am used to
it. (Grade 3)

Among those who wish for change, some wish for only small

changes ('longer playlunch, shorter lessons'; 'go home at lunch-time'). Others have in mind radical change:

> Wish the school got burnt down and we didn't go to school at all. (Grade 4)
>
> Wish I could do anything I like, and do it any time. (Grade 2)

Finally, all children do not feel equally resentful of the lack of choice. They do not all see it as based on coercion and mistrust in the way these sixth-graders do:

> Wish teachers would trust us so we can have a few different tasks to do and choose what we want to do.
>
> Wish our teachers would let us do some of what we want to do and not what she always wants to do, so we will enjoy school and not sit around sulking.

Just as there are variations in concern about choice, so also are there variations in concern about the uncertainty of not knowing 'how to do' school work. In part, this is because children vary in the extent to which they find teachers who 'show you how'. In part, it is because children vary in their dependence on teachers for all access to knowledge. This difference emerges especially in discussions of homework. Like maths, homework is something that calls for action. It is something that has to be 'done' ('I hate homework, when you can't do it, don't understand it', as one sixth-grader put it). Faced with such demands, some children have other resources they can turn to:

> I don't like teachers who give us hard projects. Like we have one on pearls and I had to ask my dad 'cause I didn't know what it was all about. (Grade 6)

Others have not:

> I can't ask my dad 'cause he didn't have much education. (Grade 4)

Finally, there are clear variations in the degree of concern with the usefulness of knowledge. While most of the children see work as distant and school in its current form as a necessary and useful prerequisite, a few display signs—even in primary school—of wishing to improve the connections in some very direct ways:

> Wish I could go to work now. (Grade 4)

Wish I could be paid for school. (Grade 5)

More about jobs, 'cause there might be about 4000 people in Queensland without work. (Grade 5)

Working things out

We shall note two differences that impressed us. One was the fluency or ease with which children came up with alternatives for current procedures in school. The other was in the degree of meaning that school held, and in the opportunities for making connections, seeing relevance, or maintaining a belief in the value of learning.

Fluency of thought. Some children readily produce innovative and nimble-witted suggestions for changing the day. Take, for instance, some of the juggling proposed for the school timetable:

> Wish I could change my maths into Epic (a curriculum package), my Epic into a book, and my book into reading time. (Grade 2)
>
> Wish school could go for an hour and fifteen minutes, and that would be big lunch and little lunch. (Grade 3)
>
> Wish we had spelling on Sunday, because then I would not be there. (Grade 3)
>
> If we had more reading, then we'd be better at spelling and creative writing. We'd probably be perfect in everything. (Grade 6)

How does such fluency of thought come about? It may be partly due to individual creativity. Its source may also lie, we suggest, in the models children encounter. Children observe teachers doing two things: treating timetables as sacred ('We must stop now because it's maths time') and treating them as moveable ('We could finish this story and do more maths tomorrow' or 'We shall have English early today because there is a special assembly'). If there are models who treat timetables as flexible, children seem likely to adopt similar ways of thinking.

The relevance of school learning. This is the form of individual difference that we wish to stress. Our interest stems first of all from noting the children's lively curiosity and their wish to learn about many things not on the usual school lists. The children's comments also point to differences in the extent to which their lives support this curiosity and maintain the sense of school as related to a real or interesting world.

Some children's lives clearly contain experiences that give particular meaning to what they wish to learn:

> More about other places. My mum and dad are Italian and they want me to learn more about other people and other countries. (Grade 4)

> More of the other language—French. I speak Vietnamese. (Grade 5)

> I'd like to learn some Greek. Like the Greek songs on television. I don't know what they are saying, so I'd like to learn a little Greek.

Such comments are a reminder to us that one child in four in Australia has one or both parents born overseas. That background gives, for many children, a particular meaning to learning about 'other places'. For the children with more local backgrounds, it also increases, the likelihood of contact with people who actually speak those 'other languages' or come from those 'other places'.

The experiences that add meaning need not be so exotic. For instance:

> More about Canberra because my aunty lives there and we're going to go down on the Christmas holidays. (Grade 3)

> More about opals and mines; we are going mining at the end of the year. (Grade 6)

> More about computers ... My mum works in the IBM and on the weekend I get her to show us into the computer room. They have this one big computer and you feed all this information to it and then all of a sudden all these machines and stuff is working and there is little boxes, one centimetre by one centimetre, and in each there is about 10 000 of them and each one contains about 50 000 of them. (Grade 3)

Looking at individual differences in terms of experiences that give meaning to school learning provides us with one way of moving towards a goal mentioned in the introduction: namely, finding alternatives to the definition of 'advantage' in terms other than money. From an experiential point of view, the lucky children are those whose own lives or whose contact with adults provides some comprehensible meaning for school learning. The unlucky are those for whom meanings are missing, either for teacher behaviour or for school learning.

The latter comment is prompted particularly by the tape from an Aboriginal school in a remote part of Western Australia. We had looked forward to reading the transcript, expecting it to add a fresh dimension to views of children's lives. To our regret, the comments on the transcript seldom came alive. When we listened to the tape, we could see why. The interviewing was carried out by a teacher who had chosen to treat it as an occasion for a formal performance in the use of English. The result was a question-and-answer period with children answering in precise turn, in complete sentences, and with answers 'sung' in a wooden and stilted fashion. The children's lack of spontaneity was probably due to the meaning—not clearly expressed, but nevertheless conveyed—given to the 'discussion' by the teacher. The tape is in strong contrast, however, to the mood of a discussion group in a hostel for Aboriginal children from several areas, where English is of necessity the lingua franca. That tape sounds very much like other discussion groups. The 'wooden' tape in the remote school was for us a vivid reminder of how children can vary in the degree and type of meaning that school learning holds for them, and in the experiences that help provide meaning.

5

FRIENDS:
a special relationship

In recent years, psychologists have developed a lively interest in asking how children define friendships, how they go about making friends and how long their friendships last[1] . What can we add?

We can add first of all some of the reasons children give for regarding friends as vitally important. To be at school—especially on the playground—surrounded by peers but without friends is 'awful'. 'You're there all alone' as one child put it. Life brightens considerably when a friend appears:

> A good friend is when you have lost all your friends and you're all alone, they just come along and chat with you. (Grade 6)

Further, to be without a friend is to be without a confidante or 'safety net' when the relationship with family turns a little sour or does not meet all your needs:

> Someone you can go to when you have just gotten into trouble with your parents, and if you have got no one to talk to you can go to your friends because they will listen to you and understand you. (Grade 6)

In addition to bringing out the reasons children give for the importance of friends, we can add some insights into the tension and drama often involved in children's friendships. On the one hand, friends are of critical importance. On the other, friends are not guaranteed. Parents and siblings may always be there but friendships have to be 'made' and 'kept'. Moreover, the rules for friendship have to be learned, and the learning is often painful. Adults may have learned subtle ways of indicating that they do not wish to start a friendship: the polite voice, the glazed eye, the scanning for opportunities to end the conversation fairly graciously. The messages children give to one another seem often to be far less subtle:

> They tell you they don't want you hanging around. (Grade 4)
>
> When you say hello, they just walk off. (Grade 3)
>
> What makes me unhappy is when you have got a friend and they say, 'I don't want to be your friend any more'. (Grade 3)
>
> One day they're your friend and the next day they say, 'Go away, we hate you'. (Grade 4)

Finally, the children's comments bring out the extent to which they are aware of the rules and conditions of friendship. They understand the opening moves:

> When someone has got a smile on their face when you meet them the first time and you say nice words then you start making friends. (Grade 2)

They accept—at least some of the time—that friendship can have its ups-and-downs:

> A good friend is someone who likes you and spends time with you and forgives you and doesn't actually bash you up. (Grade 6)

They distinguish among shades of friendship: 'friends', 'real friends', 'good friends' and 'not much of friends'. And they recognise what many psychologists have argued is an essential feature of friendships: namely, a delicate balance of exchange between relative equals, a web of sharing and obligation that rules out 'using' another person and that calls for some careful thinking about how far loyalty to one friend is compatible with an interest in others. We shall be considering a number of comments on balance and exchange. For the moment we note simply some early and later forms of awareness of sharing:

> When you have got something wrong, they help. And I give them food, so they give me food back. (Grade 2)
>
> The things that makes friends is the kindness of them. When they give you something, you feel real happy and you return the happiness and that brings out the goodness of friends. (Grade 5)
>
> If you had a good seat and they had a rusty old seat, you would give them the best seat. (Grade 2)

In this chapter we shall draw often on answers to the question, 'What makes a good friend?'. We will also incorporate comments on friendships (and enmities) which arose in the answers to questions about the liked and disliked features of school, and in the answers to five other questions: 'Who would you like to spend more time with?' 'If you were unhappy who would you go to?' 'Do you think children should have pets? Why?' 'Who thinks you are important?' 'Who are you important to?'

The frequency counts for the qualities mentioned in definitions of a good friend are shown in Table 5.1. Only those qualities mentioned by at least 3 per cent of the children are included. It should be recalled that children usually gave complex definitions ('Someone who understands you, helps you and doesn't dob you in'), and that Table 5.1 breaks up these statements, counting each quality mentioned.

We need to understand how children describe some of these features of friendship and to note where there are differences between the younger and the older children. Once again, the age changes mainly take the form of the older children using more psychological terms, referring to inner qualities, while the younger children use a language of action.

Consider first the qualities placed, in the table, under the heading of 'A caring attitude'. Constant across the grades, for

Table 5.1   The main qualities mentioned in definitions of a good friend (shown as percentages of all qualities mentioned)

	All grades	Grades 1 & 2	Grades 3 & 4	Grades 5 & 6
A caring attitude				
Likes, cares for, comforts you	23	22	25	21
Does not hit/fight	4	5	3	5
Protects, looks after you	3	5	3	5
Is available, is 'there'	3	3	2	3
Understanding and sharing				
Makes you feel special	22	19	19	26
Understands you	6	2	3	10
You understand them	6	2	5	9
Shares fun with you	19	25	24	11
Shares activities, interests, things with you	6	6	7	6

instance, is the importance of general caring and liking. (mentioned by 23 per cent of the children in grades 1 and 2, 25 per cent of those in grades 3 and 4, and 26 per cent of those in grades 5 and 6). What changes is the language of description. The first and second graders emphasise niceness and kindness, and physical care:

> When you fall over they comfort you. (Grade 1)
>
> To make a good friend you've got to be kind to other people and they'll be kind to you and that would make a good friend. (Grade 2)

The older children are more likely to give more elaborate and more psychological descriptions of caring behaviour:

> A good friend is when they like you and they are never mean to you, and respect you, and we are never fighting or scratching ourselves to death. (Grade 5)

Constant also across grades is the importance of friends not hitting or fighting you. A good friend should be:

> Someone who plays with you and sticks up for you and hardly ever bashes you up. (Grade 5)

Some of the qualities noted in the table under the heading 'Understanding and sharing' are also constant across grades. At all ages, for instance, it is important that a friend should make you feel 'special'. As we noted in Chapter 3, this is a quality that is far more prominent in expectations concerning good friends than in the definitions of a good teacher or a good parent, where presumably children learn that they have to accept a share of attention: a relatively equal share, in fact, rather than the lion's share.

What does being 'special' involve? The children's comments bring out two main components. One is that friends will be loyal. They will stand by you, and stick up for you even in the face of difficulty and temptation:

> I reckon a good friend is someone who doesn't drop you as soon as something goes wrong. (Grade 5)
>
> Well, a person that sticks by you when all the troubles come. (Grade 6)
>
> Well, I reckon if some other kids come and pick on you, then they

try and help you get rid of them; they won't leave you alone ...
and if the other kids say that they're going to bash you up, your
friend comes and actually goes up to the headmaster. (Grade 6)

Comments on loyalty in the definitions account for 9 per cent,
11 per cent, and 14 per cent of all the qualities mentioned in the
three divisions of grades.

The other component to being treated as 'special' is that the
other person will do things for you that they will not do for others.
They will, for instance, single you out as someone who is allowed
to play with their toys. Being treated as special in this way is
mentioned less often as the children grow older (9 per cent, 5 per
cent, 2 per cent). What takes its place is the sharing of secrets (1
per cent, 3 per cent, 9 per cent). A friend is increasingly defined in
terms of someone you can tell things to that you would not tell to
anyone else, someone who knows you in a way that no-one else
does:

> Someone that you tell them your secrets and they tell you theirs and
> you don't tell if they ask you not to. (Grade 5)
>
> Someone you can talk freely to. (Grade 6)

This increasing emphasis, with age, on the psychological
aspects of friendship can be seen also in the rising frequency of
references to friends as understanding you (2 per cent, 3 per cent,
10 per cent) and to your understanding them (2 per cent, 5 per
cent, 9 per cent). A friend knows how you feel and listens:

> Like when you have to do a test and your friend understands you
> and tells you not to be worried. (Grade 3)
>
> If they understand you, if you're trying to hide from your mother
> and father they will talk things over with you and might help you
> out. (Grade 4)

A friend is also easy for you to understand, and does not switch
moods in unpredictable fashion:

> Not like some people who one day they're your friend and the next
> day they punch you and kick you. (Grade 4)

The last qualities we need to note at this point have to do with
sharing. We have noted already the sharing of secrets, a form of
sharing that comes to be mentioned more and more often. Appreciated at all ages is the sharing of possessions and interests:

When they share with you and they let you take things and they let you lend things, and if things are hard for you they help you. (Grade 3)

Someone who likes to do the things you like to do. (Grade 5)

Someone with the same personality as you. (Grade 6)

Appreciated also is the sharing of fun. In fact, as we noted in Chapter 3, it is this sharing which especially distinguishes relationships with friends from relationships with teachers. It is important in all three relationships but mentioned especially often for friends.

Sharing fun does show a change with age (25 per cent of all mentions in Grades 1 and 2, 24 per cent in Grades 3 and 4, 11 per cent in Grades 5 and 6). Gradually dropping out are the simpler descriptions of friends as people who 'play with you'. Coming in at the upper levels (Grades 5 and 6) are more references to the sharing of feelings rather than only of playtimes. At all ages, though, playing together is important:

They play with you. (Grade 1)

You have lots of fun with them. (Grade 2)

Kids that play with you a lot, they make good friends. (Grade 3)

They always play with you and never gang up against you. (Grade 4)

I think what makes a good friend is that you have lots of fun with them and you can play tricks on them and they don't get angry with you. (Grade 4)

Someone who looks good and they like you and give you things and come over to your house and muck around with you. (Grade 6)

The hopes and hazards of friendship

Children's comments on family relationships brought out what they saw as the good and not-so-good aspects of family life. The mixture of positive and negative was noted also for teachers, embedded in a pattern of hopes and expectations brought to new or changing relationships. With friends, the children's comments bring out again a mixture of bright and dark moments, of features appreciated and features one would like to avoid. In describing these, we shall again look at both positive and negative aspects within the theme of hopes and expectations. We start with every child's hope that they will have some friends.

You will have some friends

Care, help, fun, understanding, company, comfort, protection, loyalty, sharing: these are the joys of friendship. It's an attractive package—no surprise, then, that children (and adults) crave friends.

At the least, the presence of some friends—good, bad or indifferent—protects against a solitary state:

> When you're all alone in the world, they just come and sit. (Grade 5)

At the best, friends seem to bring out parts of oneself that otherwise do not come fully alive. Friends, it has been suggested, are almost like part of oneself: a partial identity that only becomes fully activated when friends are present[2]. That a sense of incompleteness comes when one is without friends certainly seems to be implied in comments such as the following:

> Someone like when you are doing something and they come along and play with you and that makes you much happier. (Grade 4)
>
> I like school because of recess and lunchtime when you can have something to eat and meet your friends instead of being at home and bored at home. (Grade 6)
>
> I like playing with my friends and meeting them every morning instead of staying at home in bed. (Grade 4)
>
> At home you get bored but at school at least you have something to do and you meet friends. (Grade 5)
>
> I don't like it when we are on holidays and you don't see anyone for a few weeks. (Grade 5)

Home in these comments sounds like a grey place when you don't see 'anyone' for weeks and stay in bed for want of anything better to do. As we saw in the comments on parents, that is not children's only view of home. Nevertheless, friends do seem for some to switch on parts of the self that otherwise remain in a state of bored dormancy.

The hazards of rejection and exclusion. Aiming to have friends lays a child open to experiences of rejection and exclusion. These sometimes occur from the start ('They tell you they don't want you hanging around') but sometimes they come after an initial phase of friendly behaviour:

> Some of my friends are not very much of friends because every time I go and play with them they will be nice to me for a while and then start fighting and start pulling my hair and things and then I have to go home. (Grade 3)

> Sometimes they're your friend and other times they run off on you and they're not your friends that day. (Grade 3)

> They just go off on you ... and later they come back and all that. (Grade 6)

The exclusions or rejections that seem to be particularly hurtful are those that come when an established friendship is threatened by a third party. To have people simply 'go off on you' is bad enough. To have them abandon you for another is even more galling:

> Sometimes they'll let you play if there's no one else around, but then someone else comes along and they say, 'We don't want you' and they bash you up. (Grade 5)

> A good friend is someone who doesn't drop you when someone's got something better. (Grade 6)

> They won't let you play with someone and then they go off themselves with somebody else. (Grade 6)

It clearly takes stamina to survive these experiences and to persist in the face of a less-than-warm reception. We admired, for instance, these two children:

> I'd like to spend more time with my next door neighbour because when I go outside, he goes straight inside. (Grade 1)

> More time with my friend, because when she comes over and we go upstairs, she almost always says, 'I have to go home now. (Grade 2)

Your friends will be good company

Friends should be agreeable. To use the favorite words of the younger children, they should be 'nice' or 'kind':

> People who are nice to you and they play with you and are not nasty. (Grade 3)

> They have fun with you and they are nice to you. (Grade 6)

> Being kind and letting them play with your toys. (Grade 4)

Being nicely in love with each other. (Grade 4)

Like sometimes they're nice and they're your friend and other times they're not nice and then you aren't friends. (Grade 3)

In one group of second-graders, the interviewer, a little impatient at the string of 'someone nice' answers to her question, challenged the children to explain themselves:

I don't know ... if they keep punching and pulling your hair, they're not nice.

By contrast, the seniors struggled—without having to be prompted—to express the essence of those psychological qualities they see as important:

Someone who, instead of telling you what they want they ask you what *you* want to play. (Grade 6)

You don't have to try to be better than the other person. (Grade 6)

Someone who doesn't pick out your bad points and you won't do it to them. (Grade 5)

They don't think they are really tremendous and they are better than you at this and that. (Grade 5)

Someone trusting and who won't grab at things you say. (Grade 5)

These are fairly sophisticated criteria for friendship compared with the earlier comments.

The hazard of being 'bashed up'. It would be unusual to hear an adult define a good friend as someone who doesn't 'bash you up'. But the children often do. The phrase 'bash up' conveys its meaning so lucidly that it is used by all age groups, along with more standard English terms:

I like a friend that doesn't always fight with you and break pencils that belong to you. (Grade 4)

They're not friends when they follow you round and bother you and bash you up. (Grade 3)

Someone who doesn't play with you one day and the next day they bash you up. (Grade 5)

Getting close to people has the problem for children that it may put them in the position of possibly becoming a victim. Indeed, escaping assault is a concern at every age. Even if we discount many of the references to bashings as being in a joking vein, it still seems that there is a vast gulf between the violence level in which these children perceive themselves to be living and that commonly experienced by adults. We need to remember, however, that parents and teachers are also sometimes defined as 'good' on the grounds of their non-violence. The descriptions differ: teachers are usually described as giving the cane or the strap, and parents as belting, hitting or smacking rather than 'bashing you up'. The latter term seems to be reserved for the kinds of assault that usually come from another child. What is constant across relationships with teachers, parents and other children is the vulnerability the children feel. Getting the cane, being belted and kicked and having your pencils broken are events built into the everyday life of many children. It is not surprising that their relationships seems more stormy than those of adults, and their resentments particularly keen. How many adults feel the need to be on the alert for blows from employers, acquaintances and family members? We can only admire the self-restraint of the second-grader who ruminated that 'I don't know. . .you just don't feel like making friends with someone who keeps punching you'.

You can count on your friends

In such a turbulent world, the reliability of friends is an important quality. They should first of all 'be there':

> A good friend is someone that's reliable and somebody that's always there and somebody that won't turn their back on you and somebody that is mainly there. (Grade 5)

Friends should also be loyal and supportive. That statement seems a little bland. We need to ask as well: When are those qualities most needed? One occasion that the children note is when you are hurt or ill:

> If you've got big cuts on you, they'd probably go tell your mum, and when they come back they would being you a bandaid.
> (Grade 2)

> When you feel sick or you're down and all alone, they're just there for you to go to. (Grade 5)

A group of fourth-graders, picking up the 'sick or hurt' theme, provides some further examples:

If you fall over or get sick, they should comfort you.

They stay with you if you are very bad.

They keep you company and don't leave you.

They actually get the teacher.

Trouble does not always come from sickness or accident. Whatever the source, friends should be around to help you:

If the teacher asks you and you don't know, then they might tell you the answer and you won't get into trouble. (Grade 5)

Someone who just doesn't give up with you and helps you through your life and really cares about you like you are someone. (Grade 6)

When you're playing and somebody makes you angry they would always cheer you up and calm you down and stop you from swearing, doing something bad, stop you from hurting another person. (Grade 5)

I like someone that if you've done something wrong they'll tell you. Say if you're going to repeat it and they were scared to tell you, that you'd be too worried about it—well, like someone who can just tell you straight off just like that. (Grade 6)

Above all, the place where loyalty is needed is on the playground. It provides plenty of opportunities for loyal friends to prove themselves. They protect you from being lonely:

If you've got no-one to play with they will let you play or they will stop the game and play with you. (Grade 4)

They will also protect you from the attacks of others:

They help you and stop people bashing you up. (Grade 3)

If somebody bigger and stronger than me comes and he fights me ... then sometimes I go and tell Robert and he goes out and bashes that kid up. (Grade 4)

When everyone is annoying you and making fun of you he helps you get rid of them. (Grade 4)

Like say there's a gang of about six and you were the only one and you can't get them, they'll join you and help. (Grade 5)

Well, I reckon if some other kids come and pick on you, then they might come and comfort you and tell you not to be worried. (Grade 6)

The hazard of desertion. The children describe three common forms of desertion by friends. The first is a simple failure of physical courage:

> Like if someone was hurting you they should help you and not run away. If they run away when you get into trouble then they're not good friends. (Grade 5)

The second form of desertion is less predictable and derives from fickleness and unexplained loss of interest. In these cases the playmate abruptly 'walks off on you' or 'just goes off', leaving the deserted partner stranded:

> I like a friend you can rely on ... that won't walk away on you and that. (Grade 6)
>
> A good friend has got to be a person who'll stick with you all the time and they won't just leave you to play with someone else. (Grade 6)
>
> Well, when something happens if you fall over they shouldn't just walk away. They should help you up. (Grade 5)

A third and more complex form of abandonment involves treachery—joining the enemy. An older child provides an example:

> If you're playing with them, and say you come from a different country or like you know you're a different colour or something, well then someone else comes along and starts to tease you, and the person you're playing with doesn't want to be caught, so they start to call you names as well ... well you should be able to trust someone. (Grade 6)

The hazard of exploitation. Desertion is not the only way in which friends may be unreliable. Children turn out to be well aware that they may be exploited or 'used', to adopt the children's favourite term. Copying your work, 'blaming you when they did it', not owning up, and 'taking things when you asked them to mind them' are common forms of using, but the child most likely to be 'used' is the one with money or prized possessions:

> Like some people if you've got money, they'll use you. (Grade 6)
>
> A good friend is a person who really likes you and he doesn't use you. Like if you've got a good swimming pool or you're really rich and ... then they go off with someone else. A true friend is when they understand your problems and help you with anything that's wrong. (Grade 6).

I think a good friend should be really good to you and if you find
... like some people if you've got enough money they use you ... a
real friend understands your problems and tries to do what's right
for you. (Grade 6)

Someone who won't just hang round you. Say you say, 'I'll take you
to the movies' and you go and then when you get back he goes off
with someone else. But if he was your friend he'd stay after you
come back from the movies. (Grade 6)

Say you win the lottery and you have all these friends and when it's
all gone they just go away. Well when all the money's gone they're
friends that were their friends and they're still their friends when
the money is all gone. (Grade 5)

In each of the above examples the fairweather friends stay only
as long as the entertainment holds, thus reneging on the implicit
contract. Most of us can appreciate the difficulties inherent in any
kind of trading arrangement that calls for balancing what is given
and received. Most will also appreciate the difficulties of the
person determined not to be seen as a user, pointed to by a
fifth-grader:

You can tell if you've got a good friend. If you had something they
haven't, then they wouldn't come around.

Friends will share things with you

The discussion groups all agree that sharing is important, but
there is little consensus as to *what* is shared in an ideal friendship:

Someone who likes getting lizards together. (Grade 4)

A good friend is somebody who's been your friend for about five
years like I've got Michael. He's been my friend ever since I've been
here and he's good and we play cricket all the time and we go out
looking for the same things all the time. (Grade 5)

They sort of like the same stuff as you and you can go out on the
street and play with their friends and they'll play with your friends.
(Grade 5)

You tell them all your secrets and they tell you theirs. (Grade 6)

Each of the speakers expresses a personal interpretation. The
first two stress the sharing of interests. The third speaker has a
more expansive view—a friend is someone who has similar interests and also shares friends. The fourth emphasises the mutual
disclosure of secrets.

Sharing clearly may take many forms. On a more subtle level, it need not take the form of a completely equal exchange or a complete identity of interests. Friends need not have 'the same life as you' or 'the same ideas as you':

> I like a person you can talk to who sort of has the same ideas as you have but has got different things that they introduce you to as well. (Grade 5)
>
> I think a friend is someone who likes you, never gets bored with you and if you have got an ambition they don't just turn off and say, 'That's ridiculous' or something like that. (Grade 6)

The hazard of having one's confidence betrayed. The closer the friendship the more intimacies are exchanged, and the greater becomes the possibility of betrayal, either through breaking secrets or by 'dobbing in' ('telling on you').

> A real friend is a person you can trust and you can share your secrets and they won't whisper behind your back. (Grade 6)
>
> They would never dob on you. (Grade 5)
>
> Trust, reliability, and a person who doesn't dob on you. (Grade 6)
>
> Well, a friend that knows your problems and understands and doesn't tell on you like everyone else does. (Grade 4)

Let us first consider secrets. 'Telling your secrets' is a phrase that occurs over and over again in the interviews. Just what are these secrets? Why is telling them so important? Why is 'whispering behind your back' such a recurrent concern?

Understandably, because they *are* secrets, the children in the interviews don't detail the kinds of confidences that they have in mind. Some insight into what is going on can, however, be gleaned from studies of relationship formation in adults.[3] In moving from casual to more intimate standing, adults seem to engage in rather carefully graded and evaluated acts of disclosure about themselves. Some aspects of the self are readily offered to the most superficial of acquaintances—for instance one's name and perhaps occupation and marital status. More personal items are held back a little, and in some circumstances even asking a new acquaintance about their occupation or marital status is considered rude, because it suggests indelicate curiosity or too blatant an intention to discover the person's status in the world before wasting time in discovering what sort of person they are.

As acquaintance proceeds, private and personal information is volunteered on those occasions when it appears suitable. The rewards hoped for are of two general kinds: feelings of being understood and recognised, and feelings of increased togetherness and commitment. The associated dangers—which adults use all their accumulated social experience to guard against—are failure of understanding, rupture of the relationship, and ridicule through having one's private confessions communicated to others, perhaps for the very purpose of achieving greater intimacy with *them*.

A major problem made clear by the children's discussions is that children lack the ability to minimise the dangers of making disclosures. In particular, since any one child's own supply of secrets is likely to be quite limited, trading the elicited secrets of another ('whispering behind your back') becomes a useful means of obtaining interest and attention from others. The comment, 'They worm your secrets out of you and then talk about you behind your back' vividly describes the loser's position in this struggle for popularity.

'Dobbing' or telling tales is rather different. The disclosures here are likely to concern misdemeanours. The telling is more likely to be to authority figures (the teacher in particular) than to peers, and to result in punishment:

> I like someone who you can trust. You can always go and tell them if you've done something wrong without worrying if they're going to dob on you. (Grade 6)

> A person who trusts you and doesn't dob on you if you do something wrong. Because some people always does something wrong and the other person goes and dobs and then they belt you. (Grade 5)

Working things out: making and keeping friends

Psychologists have traditionally emphasised the importance of the earliest years of life as a time when the child comes to trust in a loving adult as a reliable source of security and understanding. The assumption has been that if all goes well in the early years, later relationships will be plain sailing. This may, in fact, be very far from the case. As we have seen, friends are not like parents: they are less tolerant of shortcomings, abhor being bored, make unreasonable demands, turn nasty, and may be seduced away by others, sometimes to join the ranks of the persecutors. Few parents (fortunately) are so hard to please. Making and keeping friends also requires many skills, some of which have to be learned away from home. For primary-schoolers, having good friends requires more than a sense of trust; indeed, the overtrusting soon learn caution. Among the most important of the skills required are:

1 Making successful overtures.
2 Learning what is expected at various stages of friendship.
3 Working out which people are unlikely candidates for friendship.
4 Deepening relationships with those seen as likely to be rewarding friends.
5 Keeping things going in a manner pleasing to both parties.
6 Making sure that each party puts a similar effort into the relationship, without keeping too close a tally.
7 Avoiding a situation where too much trust is placed in those likely to prove fickle.
8 Fighting off challenges from those who want to 'steal' friends.
9 Avoiding a situation where one is stuck with friends who no longer appeal.
10 Avoiding a reputation for disloyalty and self-seeking.
11 Avoiding a situation where one is stranded in a friendless state.
12 Achieving resilience in the face of being dumped.

Few of us, even as adults, achieve mastery of all or even the majority of these skills. It is probable that some people come to specialise in particular skills. One person might become good at selecting out the most interesting people available and 'turning on the charm', but not so good at keeping things going, and perfectly reckless about their reputation among the dumped and the elbowed-aside. Another might be a little boring, but compensate by being rock-solid loyal. A third may come to specialise in always giving a little more than is taken, thus keeping others in a state of obligation such that they cannot end the relationship without feeling guilty. To those ways of describing strategies, we might add also a distinction between using 'minimal' and 'maximal' criteria.[4] The minimal criteria strategy involves making friends with anyone who appears adequately attractive. The analogy would be with buying a dress that looks good, without looking any further for others that might look even better. Maximising involves checking out the entire available range of possibilities (friends or dresses) before making what seems the best possible choice.

Differences in skills and strategies help account for the volatility of some friendship patterns, especially when considered in combination with factors such as demands for exclusive friendship. A combination of immature social skills, minimal criteria in selecting friends, high demands for being treated as special, and the regular arrival of new parties on the scene, is a recipe for turbulence. This is a good description of the world of the primary school.

In such a situation, there will obviously be a need to work things out. We shall look at two lines of thought that children bring to our attention. The first has to do with distinguishing kinds of friendship. The second has to do with learning the rules and procedures for establishing and maintaining friendships.

Distinguishing shades and conditions of friendship

Children distinguish several shades of friendship. Some people are 'not much of friends'. Others are 'good friends' or 'best friends'. Here are some comments on the latter categories:

> Like me and Mandy, we're best friends and we always sit together and that. (Grade 3)

> A best friend is someone who likes doing what you do and thinks the same way and you're never lonely. (Grade 5)

> They're always your friend. (Grade 2)

> A good friend sticks with you and is hardly ever bored. (Grade 4)

> A best friend is someone you've known for about five years. (Grade 5)

> The old friends are my real friends, 'cause when we grow up we'll still be friends and if you need anything they might help. (Grade 6)

Children also give thought to working out who can be a friend at all. Some children obviously do not set conditions related to age, gender or other commonly adopted criteria. Their views bring out a novel approach to friendship.

> I'd like to spend more time with this man called, well he's a priest and he is called Father M...and he's really nice and he's my confession priest and he's real gentle and if you do something wrong he just goes and tells you 'Go and say some Hail Mary's or something'. (Grade 6)

> Mrs Wilson, she's an old lady she comes over to our place and she gives us lollies and when we go over to her place we're going to give her a box of chocolates. (Grade 3)

Age. For some children, however, a difference in age rules out any closeness in friendship:

> My friends out where I live, they aren't much of friends because they're bigger than me. They're alright sometimes. (Grade 2)

The problem appears to be a belief that age difference lessens the likelihood of shared interests and equal power.

Gender. Is it possible for boys in primary school to be friends with girls or vice versa? In these Australian discussion groups, the chances seem remote. All the friends mentioned are of the same gender. The few exceptions brought out some reasons for their rare occurrence or the hesitancy of children to admit their existence. One exception came in a second-grade discussion group:

> I'd like to spend more time with my girlfriend. None of you laugh—my girlfriend.

This girlfriend turned out to live in New Zealand, saving this second-grader from any day-to-day ridicule. Another second-grader was less safe. He admitted to a girlfriend with whom he would like to spend more time. A classmate then cut in to tell the interviewer that 'he has got five girlfriends' and the group burst into laughter. Second-graders are clearly aware that cross-sex friendships will be seen as romantic, and hence good for a laugh. This kind of teasing is no doubt one reason for the comparative rarity of boy-girl friendships, especially when combined with a lower likelihood of shared interests in a gender-segregated world.

Living close by. Can friends be distant, or is closeness and availability one of the conditions for making and maintaining a friendship?

Given the importance of friends 'being there' to turn to, and the lack of skill that even many adults have in maintaining friendships at a distance, it is not surprising that children at all ages consider availability as an important criterion of friendship:

Someone you play with a lot. (Grade 1)

Someone who lives close by. (Grade 2)

Sometimes they're your friends but then they might move or something and then they're not your friends. (Grade 6)

I like a friend who you can respect and play with all the time whenever you're available...because if you got friends that they hardly ever let you play with them they're not your real friends. (Grade 6)

Kids that play with you a lot, they make good friends. If they don't play with you much they're not very good because you don't get to see them much, and then you actually don't like them. They're good friends when they come over to your house and if they don't wreck anything. If they wreck something well they're not very good friends. (Grade 3)

Special skills or intense attachments appear to be needed if friendships are not to wither on the vine once friends move away or have less time to spend with you. It is an unusual child who says that physical closeness is not all that necessary:

A good friend doesn't have to be around you a whole lot, just be understanding and helpful. (Grade 6)

Pets. For some children, pets clearly fill a number of the criteria for being friends. You can share fun with them and talk to them:

I would like to spend more time with the animals and with me friends because with your friends you can play games and with your dogs you can take them for a walk. (Grade 6)

My dog is a good friend because we play with him all the time and he jumps on me. (Grade 2)

My dog, she's beautiful as a person 'cause when you say 'Sit' she doesn't sit and when you say 'Come on', she does. (Grade 5)

I like to be with my cocky because he sits on your sholders and says your name and there's no need to say 'What?'. (Grade 6)

Pets may also play the role of comforter and confidant. Pets may, in fact, be seen as better than other people in this role, because they ask so little in return. The problem of fair exchange in relationships is automatically overcome. There are no betrayals, no taking sides, no bursts of moral disapproval, no tantrums or sudden attacks. When asked what they did when they were unhappy, about 15 per cent of children made some mention of pets:

> When you are lonely cats can make you happy. When they are trained well, it's sort of like a person. (Grade 4)

> I go and talk to my dog because they don't get angry with you. (Grade 2)

> I go to the dirt track and I go to my chicken cage and talk to my rooster. (Grade 6)

> I just lie on the bed with the cat and we remember all the good things I have done. (Grade 3)

> I go and talk to my next door neighbour's dog or her budgerigars. (Grade 5)

> I go to my goats. (Grade 2)

As these comments indicate, a high degree of attentiveness is not important. Budgerigars, mice, roosters, horses and goats all fill the role of confidante adequately. Cats and dogs, however, do appear especially responsive:

> My cat—whenever I'm unhappy he comes up and he licks me and sits next to me. (Grade 4)

> If it was at school I would talk to my friends and if it was at home I would try to talk to my dog because she understands English. (Grade 5)

> I go down to the paddock under a tree and I let Robin out and we just sit there and think about it. (Grade 6)

Learning the skills of friendship

From among the many skills that friendships require, we shall draw out some related to two phases: starting a friendship, and maintaining one in the face of disagreements and jealousy. The children are perceptive about the activities and problems involved in each phase, even at an early age.

Starting a friendship. For all of us, the phrase 'making friends' has real meaning. Parents and siblings may simply 'be there'. One may wish that 'my brother got born into some other family' but his going away is unlikely. Friends are another matter. Parents and siblings may help you get started, but you have to follow through by your own actions, by being 'friendly' or by taking on whatever the obligations your social group has established for friendship. When parents and siblings are not around to introduce you to other children, getting started is even more of a problem. It is, in

fact, the activity mentioned by some children as what they don't
like about school:

> Meeting people. (Grade 3)

> I don't like people teasing me in big classes and I don't like making
> friends. (Grade 3)

What are the skills needed for starting friendships? And how
much awareness do children show of what is needed?

For the first question, we may draw on a study by two American
psychologists[5]. They noted that popular children were especially
good at gaining entry into small groups of other children. They
were particularly good at noting what the group was currently
interested in, and then establishing themselves as sharing this
interest or as having something to offer. In a further study,
Gottman listened to the conversations of four- and five-year-olds
and found that some of these children were adept at starting
friendships by offering information—'telling secrets' about themselves or their family.[6]

The children in our discussion groups show an awareness of
several strategies. The following were suggested by second
graders:

> When they are new to the school you show them around.

> You can make friends when someone falls over and you go and
> take them to the teacher or to the sick bay and you can become
> friends.

> When you haven't got anyone to play with and you are sad and you
> are sitting down on the seat all by yourself and someone comes up
> and says 'Would you like to play with us?'.

> When somebody comes out of the shop and they didn't have any
> money, you give them some money.

> When new people come on our bus, you sit next to them and you
> make good friends.

For these second-graders, finding an acceptable means of
establishing contact is the issue. They appear confident that the
rest will follow. By third grade, however, the children are more
likely to be conscious that relationship formation is helped by
following certain rules and rituals:

> Well, to make a good friend you should ask them your name and

what are you and what grade you're in and then they get to play with you and then they like you. (Grade 3)

When you first meet him you spend more time with him and sit next to him in class. (Grade 5)

Someone who lets you do models and if you don't wreck them and then you let them do some of your models and then you gradually get more companionship and then you gradually get friends. (Grade 4)

Maintaining a friendship. From an early age, children are aware that *exchange* is a feature of friendships. Among younger children especially, the exchange is often expressed in material terms:.

He's my friend because he gives me icy poles. (Grade 1)

Sharing, giving lollies to each other. (Grade 2)

They look after you and swap food with you. (Grade 3)

They let you play with their toys. (Grade 2)

A good friend is like when he buys you something like an ice-cream or something and then you buy him something. (Grade 2)

The exchange need not always be immediate:

If you told them something in trust they wouldn't tell anybody and if I was running out of money they would lend me some and I'd always pay them back and give them money if they needed it. (Grade 5)

Nor need it always be material

Jason, he's one of my friends who goes to a different school and he doesn't let anyone come over to his house 'cause they wreck all his toys, but he lets me come over sometimes 'cause I haven't broke anything so far and he wants more companionship. (Grade 3)

In this case careful behaviour and companionship are being traded for the rare privilege of entry to the home and toys of the exclusive Jason. In other cases, the exchange is more one of respect for each other's interests and feelings:

Like if I say, 'Let's go swimming today' and he says, 'No' and he wants to go somewhere else and I say, 'We'll go next Saturday where you wanna go and we'll go swimming now'. (Grade 6)

Someone who listens to you, someone who cares, like if you care about him and he cared about you. (Grade 6)

If you want to play cricket and they agree, and they suggest playing something that you don't really like but you still play it anyway and they do vice-versa. (Grade 6)

Children thus see the maintenance of a reasonable exchange as an important part of keeping a friendship going. Two other tricky aspects of maintaining a relationship emerge in the children's comments. One has to do with arguments or fights, the other with jealousy.

Arguments between friends require some special handling and some fine points of distinction. There are children who consider that good friends should not fight at all:

I reckon what makes a good friend is that they are always on your side and they never fight with you and whenever you need them they're there. (Grade 4)

A far larger group considers that a friendship should be able to sustain some conflict, provided that it is handled in particular ways:

They are good friends if you get in a fight and at the end of the fight in one second you're friends again. (Grade 2)

Someone you can trust or they'll trust you and you can have fights with them, but not punching fights. You'll make up with them and you won't stay enemies with them for ages. (Grade 5)

You do have fights...but they always come back to you. (Grade 5)

The most perceptive advice was offered by a sixth-greader:

You need patience with friends. They're hard to get along with sometimes.

The friend in mind may well have been a sixth-grader such as the following:

CHILD: What makes me unhappy is when I fight with my best friends and when I do something wrong.

INTERVIEWER: What is terrible about fighting with other people, what makes you feel so bad about that?

CHILD: You say awful things to all your friends and you should be saying good things to them.

Fair exchange and limited arguments: these are two proposed ways of maintaining friendships. A third way has to do with ways of coping with third parties and jealousy.

Particularly in school settings, where peers are all around you, the presence of third parties often calls for considerable finesse. On the one hand, friends expect loyalty. On the other hand, they themselves wish to make new friends and not to be stranded. The possible complications are many. Some children, for instance, report having a 'reserve' best friend, for those occasions when the primary best friend is away or is temporarily alienated, usually as a result of some dispute as to who shall get their own way. In these cases, the children seem to be trying to do three things simultaneously: keep the primary 'best' friendship going; test and perhaps advance their own power position within it, thus putting it at risk; and maintain a fall-back relationship with a less demanding but less interesting third party. When a number of classmates are all playing these games, small wonder that friendships are both an exciting and dangerous arena.

What should a good friend do when someone new appears on the scene? None of the children propose that you should take no interest, or that jealousy should never be felt. What they propose once more is a set of limits within which this behaviour should fall. The first friend should not simply be abandoned:

> Someone who doesn't just drop you because there is someone new. (Grade 5)

> Say if you were playing with them and someone else came along they wouldn't go off with them. (Grade 6)

> The only good friends I know are kind and friendly and don't stop playing with me and don't run off on me and don't go and play with someone else. (Grade 4)

More subtly, the signs of interest displayed in a new person or the signs of jealousy should be kept to a minimum:

> A good friend...like for one little thing they might get jealous but that's alright so long as they don't take it really bad. (Grade 6)

> I think a good friend is like if you have a friend and another person comes new to the school...they talk to them but they don't look away from you and they don't go with them. (Grade 6)

In short, children display in their discussions of friendship the same forms of working things out that they display when discussing the exercise of control and discipline by parents and teachers. The simplest line of thought is to argue that painful events should not happen. In practice, the children come to accept that they do, and proceed to work through the problems at hand.

Individual differences

In previous chapters, we have considered two kinds of individual differences: differences in the way children work things out, and differences in the balance of positive and negative features in a particular aspect of their life. We will look at children's friendships in the same way.

Working things out

We have referred throughout to a change, with age, in the language of description children use and in the degree of emphasis on concrete or material aspects of relationships ('they give you things', 'they take you places', 'they play with you') as against internal qualities ('they are patient and understanding'). With increasing age, children also move from a black-and-white view of the world ('friends should never fight with you') to a view that contains some shades of grey and some tolerance for human failings.

Naturally, some children stand out as being more perceptive or more articulate about inner states than others of the same age. We have in mind, for instance, the sixth-grader who described as one of the main requirements of friendship, 'patience' because 'they're hard to get along with sometimes'. That view is reminiscent of the perspective offered by another sixth-grader commenting on teachers: 'You've got to give it to them to have some bad days'. Both children display an unusual ability to refrain from indignation, to take the other person's point of view, and to be tolerant of imperfections.

Another interesting form of individual differences has to do with the extent to which a setting provides children with explanations as to why they are rejected or excluded. For some children, being 'dropped' can remain a mysterious affair. The children who made the following comments didn't seem to feel the need to explain the strange ways in which they were treated.

I'd like to spend more time with my next door neighbour because when I go outside he goes straight inside. (Grade 2)

My friend, because when she comes over and we go upstairs, she almost always says, 'I have to go home now'. (Grade 2)

Explanatory work is hardly necessary when others make it quite clear to you why you are not wanted:

They call you a wog. (Grade 3)

They chase after me and call me 'Fatty Fin'. (Grade 2)

I like someone who is not hard on you because most kids usually think if someone is pretty, well they go after them, but when you are not pretty... (Grade 3)

In these cases, the child has to struggle with the notion that the problem is associated with something very personal. Among children, it seems to be fairly standard that any explanations for rejection offered by peers will be of this 'all your fault' kind. Does it matter? Like the children who see problems at school arising because they are 'dumb' or difficulties in the morning as caused by their being 'slow', the task of solving problems and maintaining self-esteem becomes all the harder when explanations of the 'your fault' or 'your problem' kind are all that is offered to you. A child has to work a little harder to come up with the kind of statement we admired from a second-grader:

I am not big, but I are strong and I are sexy.

The balance of pleasures and problems

The children's comments bring out a phenomenon often discussed in studies of friendships. Some children are 'stars': they appear to receive and give pleasure through many friendships.

I'd like to spend more time with Tracey. Everyone wants to be her friend. (Grade 5)

More time with Sonia. She's real special. If the girls have a problem, they all go to Sonia. (Grade 5)

Everyone likes Mark. (Grade 4)

Less often discussed are some individual differences especially related to the problem of negative peer group pressures. Consider, for instance, the child who experiences—through friendship—the pressure to behave in a way which might go against the principles with which he has been brought up. A fifth-grader provides an example:

> CHILD: Some kids get into trouble. The hang around with other kids who go into shops and steal things, and then they steal things too and get into trouble.
>
> INTERVIEWER: But do they have to go with the bad kids? Couldn't they stay away?
>
> CHILD: But not if it's their friends.

One of the pleasures of friendship which children experience to different degrees is the way in friends can act as a 'safety net'. They may provide a way of redressing the balance when things are not going well at home or at school:

> I'd like to spend more time with my friend Peter, because my parents are separated and Peter is sort of like a father to me and he makes me feel real happy. (Grade 4)

An especially memorable comment was the following:

> Linda, I told her about my family problems and she sort of understands me all the time. Like when I go and tell mum all she says is, 'Oh go on, it doesn't hurt, does it?' Linda is a good friend because she knows all the details about my family and she understands me when I've got a problem and everything like that. Whenever I've got a problem I always turn to Linda. We never have a secret apart; like if I'm going somewhere I'll tell Linda and if Linda is going somewhere she'll tell me.

The friendship described here is not the same as the usual relationship with a parent. (None of the discussions of parents refer to 'never having a secret apart'). The friend is seen here as more understanding and more reliable than the parent, a perception which may be influenced by the fact that the child who made the comment was at the time under foster care. In such cases, friends like Linda are clearly life-savers. One's only reservation is that the relationship used to offset the family shortcomings may not be the sturdiest of substitutes. Children's friendships appear to change rapidly; the demands on Linda seem large; and the child may come to regret that Linda 'knows all the details about my family'. For the moment, however, it is clear that the child who has such a safety net—and can provide care and understanding in return—is 'advantaged', regardless of other apparent inadequacies in her (or his) life.

6

SOME GUIDELINES
FOR CHANGE

Our effort to understand what home and school mean to children would be incomplete unless we attempted to answer the question: How can we use our perceptions to improve children's lives? Our hope throughout has been to use our understanding of children to help guide our decisions concerning their lives, and to break down the distance often felt between adults and children.

Our main suggestion is this: note the children's own proposals for change, presented in each of the chapters. From this point, each family or teacher may find it best to take their own steps forward. We offer some ideas that may help point the way. All of these ideas are related to the framework we have adopted and developed throughout the several chapters. A quick summary of that framework will perhaps be in order to refresh the memory.

Briefly, we have started from Bronfenbrenner's proposal that the world we live in consists of several settings, each marked by particular activities and particular relationships.[1] The settings may be places: home, school, playground, office, factory. They may also be states: being a preschooler, being single, being married, being part of a new friendship. Life consists of time spent within a setting and of transitions between settings: transitions that may be daily experiences of entry and re-entry (home to school and back again, for instance) or major changes (becoming a school-child, becoming a parent, emigrating, changing houses or jobs) which occur only once or a few times in a lifetime.

A basic goal in life is to be comfortable and effective in each setting. Another basic goal—less often recognised—is to cope with transitions. None of us remains in one setting all our lives, even if the only change is from the state of being younger to the state of being older. We hope for transitions that will be smooth and a source of pleasure rather than being abrupt, frightening or disappointing, transitions that will open up new options rather than closing doors and creating a sense of loss.

A third goal—underlined for us by the children's stress on sharing and understanding—is for continuing links between people. My world and yours need to come together; my experiences need to have some meaning to you and yours to me; my feelings need to be understood by you and yours by me. Without such sharing and mutual understanding, there is a threat of feeling isolated: separate and apart from others, or at odds with them.

What promotes the achievement of these goals? Maas has proposed—in an analysis influenced by Bronfenbrenner—that we aim in any setting to *build in access, options, and control*.[2] In his view, the degree to which these features are present marks the difference between one setting and another and alters the likelihood that people will feel satisfied with their experiences in any setting. Our suggestions are similar but in slightly different terms: *build useful links, help children make sense of events, and reduce the 'cost' of the benefits to be gained from a setting.*

To make those suggestions more specific, we shall look separately at the home and school settings. The two, of course, are closely related to one another and the ways of improving one are often similar to ways of improving the other.

The home setting

Building links

In the home setting, the links that the children talked about most were links between people and between past and present.
Links between people. With some people in our lives, the sense of shared experience is strong. We have grown up together, read the same books, worked together, faced trouble together. There is a sense of 'we-ness'. It takes relatively little effort for each person to understand the majority of the other's experiences. A close relationship, a tightly-knit family, a traditional society, the shared experience of war: these settings promote such links.

Children seek such a sense of togetherness. In day-to-day terms, how does it come about?

The most direct route is through doing things together. Children make it clear that these shared activities do not have to take the form of grand occasions that require major preparation. The sense of links may be strongest with small acts: 'just sitting talking', 'doing things together', 'eating together'. One of the most telling illustrations of this point was contained in the remarks of the two children who said that the best parts of overseas holidays were when the family sat around together working out what they would do, or stayed up late talking.

Doing things together is a very direct route to the sense of a shared world. The experience of one person is very much a part of the experience of the other. What threatens it?

One threat is that time spent together is not always a shared activity. You may work side by side without any sense of doing something together, or with only the sense that you are doing what you are ordered to do. Another threat is that some people, although they are around, don't *join in*. One—usually mum—is locked into 'caring' activities and 'doesn't play'. The other—usually dad—is always doing big jobs or resting from them, and doesn't share in the day-to-day opportunities for working together.

Both those problems can be reduced. We can all join in rather than stand on the sidelines. We can all aim at building into activities and tasks the feeling of a joint enterprise in which children are allies, making a useful contribution. There is, however, no way in which people can always be physically together, doing things together. One or both parents go off to work. Children go off to school (a break in physical togetherness that the children comment on far more often than on parents' departures for the paid work force). Parents and children have 'outside interests': friends, sports, hobbies, social groups. All told, a life of total physical togetherness is simply not a possibility. It might not even be wished for.

The important consequence of this physical apartness is that *links have to be constructed*. That problem surfaces at all ages. Who has not been bored by the accounts of some one else's vacation in a place one has never seen? Who has not given up on the task of explaining to someone else what an experience was really like? The problem is simply larger between adults and children because the experiences are more likely to be separate.

Ways need to be found to help bridge differences in experience, making what happens to one person real to the person not there. This is often more easily said than done. The children's basic suggestion is that parents, if they can't join in, should '*take an interest*'. We have come more and more to see the significance of even brief visits to the other's setting, with an eye open for features and people to be discussed or asked about later. We have also come to realise the value of phone calls, postcards, routine notes about 'where I'll be today', stories that make things real and bring in a family member ('You would have liked something I saw today'; 'I thought of you when I heard ...'; 'What happened to me today made me really sympathise with the time when you ...', 'Remember when you came to the office and ... well, today ...'), as well as family bulletin boards with pictures and other reminders of settings where various family members spend time.

Most of all, 'taking an interest' seems to call for mastering some of the arts of conversation. It is easy to be trapped into questions that invite a simple 'yes' or 'no' and lead nowhere. Conversations with children often take the form: 'What did you do today?'— 'Nothing'. As in all continuing conversations, we need to work at specific leads and specific links to past conversations: 'What happened about ... ?'; 'Did Y. come?'; 'How did that trouble about Z. work out?'; 'How did you (or someone else) feel about that?'. Some of us live with people who make it easy to 'take an interest', who tell all given the slightest prompting. Most of us have to work a little harder at the job, making use of every available prop—from workbooks to class pictures and scraped knees—to bridge the distance between one person's direct experience and another's indirect knowledge, creating a sense of togetherness out of the two.

Links between past and present. The need to construct links applies also to what children see as another good part of family life: the sense of being part of a larger, continuing group. The lives of certain distant relatives and the past lives of parents are not immediately accessible to children. They may be made more real by spending more time with those rarely-seen relatives, or by actually seeing the places where parents lived in earlier times. However, most of the links between past, present and future have to be constructed: constructed by children or for them.

With this is mind, we have begun to look more closely at stories about more distant times, places, and people, asking: Are these links made in terms that children will understand and find interesting?

The question has brought out for us the value of telling stories about people and the past in ways that relate to the child's interests, that bring them into the picture, that place them as members of a group but still respect their individuality ('Your grandparents would have liked to have seen that'; 'That's your Aunt Susan—some people think that you and she look a little alike'; 'One reason you are named ... is because ...'). Those suggestions may sound as if they promote a self-centred view on the part of the child. Few of us, however, are interested in stories to which we cannot relate.

In short, we might do well to choose or construct stories that show children where they fit or belong, and that link past events to what children themselves experience. Think about what you remember from your own parents' stories of the past, and see if these memories support our theory.

What about the child's own past and future? Pictures of the child as a baby, drawings made in kindergarten, first attempts at writing: all these are useful props for reconstructing the past. The future is often more difficult to make real. For children, the link they most often note is the continuing presence of the same caring group of people. The future needs relatively little thought when one has the assurance that your parents 'will look after you all your life'. It is the loss or threatened loss of that bridge—in the face of feeling small, relatively powerless, and ignorant of what lies ahead—that gives young children a particular concern about events such as divorce, war or hospitalisation: 'What will happen to me?' Where there is a threat to that parental link with the future, it would seem wise to make it clear that the future caring will exist even though certain aspects of life may change.

Links between family and friends. We have been emphasising the development of links and of mutually understood experiences among family members. Many of the same points apply to friends. Children clearly enjoy the sense that friends can come to your house and that you can go to theirs. If we are hesitant in going beyond that statement, it is because the children's comments point up some hazards they see in this particular forging of links. One is that the linking may not be successful: 'It's no fun going to Mike's house because his mother doesn't let us do hardly anything'. The other is that the linking may threaten one of the important qualities of friends, namely that their special relationship is to *you*: not to your parents or to your siblings or to any other attractive people they meet through you. The relationship is threatened when the introduction is to someone who then 'takes your friend over'. Part of the special relationship is also your ability to disclose information about yourself at a pace and in a form that fits a sense of mutual exchange and mutual disclosure. Parents or siblings who 'tell all about you' are not simply 'embarrassing': they are a threat to the delicate development of mutuality in friendship. Parents can diminish this threat both by being careful in their own conversations with the child's friends, and, by exercising control over the disclosures of siblings.

Helping to make sense of things

At all ages in life, we feel more comfortable when the events around us make sense, when they can be given meaning. This simple fact underlies the effort psychologists put into studying people's explanations: explanations for success or failure, for illness or accident, for the way people behave. Children, as we have seen, work hard at making sense of their experiences, putting together the best picture they can out of whatever materials are available. What role can adults play in the child's explanations? The children's comments lead to two suggestions.

Ask: What's hard to understand? To judge by the children's comments, the area calling for most mental effort in the home setting is the exercise of parental control and discipline. As one child said, 'They growl at you and then they say they growl at you because they love you, and it doesn't make sense'. As many of them said, the good parent is one who explains why you can't have something but 'doesn't go on and on about it'. The children are not asking for a lack of parental control. They accept that it is the parents' task to teach them 'right from wrong' and to see that they follow established rules. To make good sense, however, the rules have to be clear and the consequences of doing wrong must be appropriate. In the words of a second-grader, 'They yell at you when you're naughty, but only when you're naughty'. In the words of another, 'Telling you is enough'.

Ask: What explanations are you offering? What type of explanations are best avoided? In daily life, we not only work out explanations for ourselves; we also offer them to others. Consider just a few: 'I forgot'; 'I've had a hard day'; 'He didn't mean it'; 'She was really trying to help'; 'Boys don't do that'; 'Those are not nice people'; 'You could try harder'.

Adults have a responsibility to offer some explanations of events and behaviour, especially when children could come up with unhappy explanations if left to their own devices. Adults also have a responsibility to offer reasonable explanations. For what might be 'reasonable', we shall be guided by the children's comments and by some of the developmental literature. The explanations should be short (don't 'go on and on') and concrete (don't create more mystery than before if you can help it). They should reflect the child's right to ask (to say you find something hard to explain is better than to imply that the child should not be thinking or asking about such things). And they should avoid leaving the child with the feeling that the situation is hopeless: that the causes lie in something that cannot be changed, about which nothing can be done, and towards which the only possible reaction is one of helplessness.

The explanations we would most like to see avoided are those that place the responsibility for problems on the child, with the implication that no change is possible: 'You're ungrateful'; 'You're spiteful'; 'You just take after . . .'. A more valuable form of comment is in the following vein: 'I see you're the kind of person who likes to help (or who has a sense of humour, really tries, bounces back, thinks about other people). The comment helps construct a continuing identity. Use such statements sparingly, is Grusec's advice.[3] They can backfire or lose effectiveness if used too often. And use them only for behaviour of which you and the child are proud. To be constantly told that one is mean, rude, or untidy constructs a negative picture for both parent and child. In these cases, a reference to the specific and to the here-and-now ('That was rough'; 'Your room's untidy') constructs a picture that does not link past, present and future together in a way that leaves no hope for improvement.

The other explanations to be avoided are those implying that parents 'don't care' (or that they 'don't care as much for me as they do for X.'). Most parents are sensitive to the significance for children that parents 'care'. They may even go to great lengths to explain their behaviour in terms of how much they care. For children to lose confidence in their parents' caring attitude is a major loss. They need to feel that 'If you fall off waterskiing, they will come back for you'; 'If you are late coming home, they will come to look for you'; 'If you are in trouble, they will listen'; 'When you are sick, they will look after you'; 'They're proud of you if you win, but if you don't, they don't mind'. They also need to feel, even more than they come to feel with friends, that some 'bad' behaviour will not mean a loss of caring. It can mean a loss of privilege but should not mean a loss of love or of the bedrock confidence that—especially. in this young and vulnerable stage— you will be loved and cared for.

Reducing the 'cost' of family happiness

The joys of any setting come at the cost of effort, patience, a share of the work, a readiness to consider someone else's point of view, a willingness to hold one's tongue. Some of these tasks are more problematic than others. The children's comments point to four aspects that might well be considered in reducing some of the more problematic ones.

A readable script. Family life is much like participating in a play. It helps if there is a script that all understand, with a clear sequence of events and a clear set of instructions as to who does what and what changes are possible.

A little choice. We notes in Chapter 2 how many of the children's wishes took the form: 'I wish I could . . .', 'I wish I didn't have to . . .'. We might well argue that children have to learn that some things have to be done, and that all must take a share of the work. But it should also be possible to build in some element of choice in what one does. One child, for instance, suggested that 'They should decide what has to be done, but we can decide when to do it'. That form of working things out may not be effective for all families, but some input from children and some contribution from them in the decision-making would relieve the sense of compulsion and lost options.

Less time pressure. Most adults have become so used to having their lives run by the clock that if often takes a while to realise that 'learning to live with the clock' is a major part of growing up in our society. We now see that adjusting to clock-time is an important aspect of the switch from being at home to being at school, including the experience of getting ready for school in the mornings. It is also a large part of the joy of vacations and of 'relaxed' weekends. Small wonder that sociologists such as Berger see a preoccupation with clock-time as one of the signs of 'modernity'[4], and that the people labelled 'counter-culture' often refuse to wear a watch.

Once again, it is easy to argue that some of this learning is needed: children need to learn 'respect for time'. We would add the questions: When is a concern for clock-time really necessary? Where can it be softened? How far has living by the clock become such a virtue in itself that we extend it into areas where it is not really necessary? These primary-school children clearly question much adult concern with clock-time. We could perhaps learn something from their approach.

Less interference from siblings. Among the children, approximately half of the views expressed about siblings were negative. If we were to interview parents, it seems likely that at least half would place arguments between siblings as one of the 'costs' of family life that they could do without.

While acknowledging the difficulties involved, we would like to draw attention to the value of creating a sense of alliances and common causes. Such positive aspects of sibling relationships emerged in many of the children's comments, and their value is reinforced in Dunn and Kendrick's finding that sibling friction was reduced by the older sibling being helped to feel some sense of partnership with parents in the care of a new child.[5]

Again, while recognising the difficulties, we would suggest that the goal might be one of keeping sibling friction within limits rather than eliminating it altogether. That proposal comes in part from the children reminding us that some parts of sibling friction can be 'fun' and can be useful practice in assertion. Children may often 'stir' or 'walk their wits' more safely with siblings than with friends who might reject them completely because of their behaviour. The children's comments also reminded us that sibling friction often indicates real problems. Siblings do present some special forms of interference. They may interfere with relationships with parents, standing in the way of one's own special claims. They may also link settings and experiences in ways one does not like: the sibling who tries to finish a younger child's stories because he or she 'said it all before' is often the kind of person one prefers not to have around. In such cases, a parent may be able to minimise sibling friction by explaining the problems of interfering in this manner.

The school setting

As with the home setting, we shall look at ways of constructing useful links, helping children to make sense of events, and reducing the 'cost' of the benefits to be gained from the setting.

Building links

The links we have in mind are between home and school, between school and the 'real world', between past, present and future, and between peers.

Links between home and school. Children often face the transition to school life (or from one grade to another) with only the smallest pieces of information, perhaps with only the vague assurances that 'you will enjoy school' or that 'things get really interesting in grade ...'

The transition to school life, and the links between home and school, have been of special concern to Bronfenbrenner.[6] He has pointed specifically to the value of information for parents and of person-to-person links for children (visits by both parents and child to the school, direct meetings with the teacher who will be the child's main point of contact once in school). To those suggestions, we may add others that have a similar linking value: work brought home and appreciated (for example, drawings or paintings), pictures of teacher and class (worth placing on a bulletin board as a prop to conversation rather than being placed in a rarely-viewed album). We would draw attention also to the recognition that some things must be left at home (must everything be?) and that some things have to be remembered. How can we help children develop routines so that they rarely have to say, 'I hate it when I leave my pencils or my homework behind:'. How can we work towards the links between home and school being comfortable ones? All the settings we inhabit have some effect on one another. They are never completely separate, and children generally need to be reassured about the nature of these links.

Links between school and the 'real world'. In Chapter 4 we made the point that a great deal of school learning is out of context. Dinosaurs, cavemen, history: these belong to past time and can only be read about. Harbours, coal mines, transport systems, living animals: these belong to present time but are still mainly read about. Small wonder that the children enjoy excursions, films, fashion shows, cooking, plays, sport.

It may well be argued that some learning must be second-hand, and that school has a large part to play in helping us cope with learning in this style.[7] In time, we hope that children will learn how to construct some links of their own between classrooms and 'real' life. In the meantime, why does so much of the school curriculum need to be concerned with distant topics or to deal in a remote fashion with topics where some direct experience is possible?

Links between present and future. Most children have only the vaguest notions about the relationship between school and later adult life. At least in primary school, they take it on faith that going to school and 'doing well' will protect them from growing up 'dumb' and unable to get a job. Given the length and sometimes the weakness of the chain between school and paid work, there seems little point in belabouring this connection during primary school. In secondary school, however, the information needs to be more to the point; evidence abounds that children and their parents do not always have a clear picture (or access to a clear picture) of future options and of the many ways in which school is related to these.[8]

More easily comprehensible for primary school children are transitions from grade to grade. For these changes, and for transitions from teacher to teacher, it is worth asking: What information are children given? What information do they generate for themselves? The latter question is prompted by a telling anecdote in Davies' book on children's accounts of life in primary school.[9] A new teacher has arrived. What would he be like? What could they expect? Anxious to know and to prepare themselves before actually being in class, several children made a quick, uninvited inspection of the classroom before assembly. The look of the classroom—desks in rows, work already written neatly on the board—were for them all the evidence they needed. This would be a teacher who liked 'a line down the margin of the page'.

Links between daily activities. The day at school includes many shifts from one activity to another: from English to maths, from work to sport, from listening to writing, from one set of pages to another. These transitions are often felt by children to be arbitrary. They occur 'just when you're getting going' or 'just when you've got to the good part'. They are also signalled in ways that are not always clear: 'In a few minutes ...'; 'Now, class ...'; 'Right ...'; 'O.K., now'. We might well ask ourselves: What signals are we giving? Are they clear? Are the moments of transition too arbitrary?

Links between peers. One of the hopes of adults is that they will be able to help children build comfortable and rewarding relationships with each other. To this end, psychologists often ask how one encourages the development of social skills in children, and what relationships exist between ideas and actions: between, say, a child's understanding of the rules of friendship and a child's popularity?

Teachers might see themselves as having little or no responsibility for helping to build these links. Children have a different view. They appreciate teachers who foster links among children, not only by refraining from having 'favourites' but also by more positive action:

> A good teacher makes us feel like a class. We do things together. (Grade 5)
>
> When you are new, she sees you have no-one and she takes someone over, and you become friends. (Grade 2)

Helping to make sense of things

The questions suggested as being useful with regard to the home setting can also be applied to help make sense of things in the school setting.

Ask: What's hard to understand? Mehan has pointed out that children need to learn the meaning of many teachers' statements[10]. They need to learn, for example, what they are supposed to do when the teacher says, 'Who can tell me...:?'. The invitation is not to say, 'I can' or to give the answer, but to raise one's hand.

The children we have listened to bring out some other puzzling behaviour displayed by teachers. Some of this behaviour, as with parents, has to do with the exercise of control and discipline. Teachers are expected to be in control, but to exercise power in ways that are 'fair'. What children find hard to understand is the use of power in inconsistent, excessive, or demeaning ways. Why do teachers hit, yell, 'chuck mentals', tell you you're a fool, punish the whole class, send you outside where you won't learn anything?

A second area of puzzlement has to do with teachers' moods. Without expecting teachers to always have sunny dispositions, it is amazing to the children that teachers are so often 'grumpy'. Above all, it is strange that they become so angry when 'all you've done is not understand'. 'Why don't they just explain?' is a constant cry.

Ask: What explanations are being offered?; What type of explanations are best avoided? Children's explanations come from themselves, their peers, and their teachers.

The easiest explanations (and the kindest to oneself) place the responsibility on teachers. They 'won't explain'; 'They've forgotten what it is like to be young'; 'They don't care'; 'They're not fair'; 'They don't like children'; 'They don't enjoy teaching'.

In contrast, the explanations teachers offer (according to the children) place responsibility within the children. 'You didn't listen'; 'You didn't try'; 'You have to figure things out for yourself'.

Chapter 3 gave a reasonably full account of this tug-of-war for the explanations that will prevail. We shall note here—as we did for parents—the importance of avoiding explanations that are derogatory and that offer no hope for change or improvement.

More productive are explanations that hold out hope and suggest a way forward: 'Let's try a different way'; 'Let's see how the work goes when things settle down'; 'Put more spaces between the lines', rather than 'Your work's untidy'; 'You need to practise this particular part'. The basic goal, it has often been said, is to avoid a state of feeling helpless, writing off the possibility of change because of some personality trait or behaviour pattern thought to be at fault.

Reducing the 'cost' of learning

Children pay a price for learning, a price that is often high. Many of the problematic parts of the cost involved are similar to those we noted in the home setting: a script that is hard to follow, little choice in what one does, a day ruled by the clock and a year ruled by the calendar, and the unavoidable company of people who do not always have your interests at heart or treat you kindly.

Many of these negatives could be reduced. We would argue especially—given the vehemence of some of the children's comments—for the need to find ways of having children feel less confined to the prison of the classroom. Even more strongly, we would argue for the need to find ways of introducing some sense of choice and some sense of the children's influence over the work that is done. Choice and influence are issues which are clearly dear to the hearts of children, though they express these terms in a much simpler and more concrete form. These issues should also be important to adults if they wish to see children playing an active and effective part in life.

A last word: taking the child's perspective

This book has, of course, been chiefly concerned with the child's perspective: we have looked at children's views on the best and the hardest parts of their activities and relationships, their views on the difference between one setting and another, their notions of how things are related to one another, their suggestions for how things might be improved. We have learned a great deal from simply reading the children's own comments, and we hope that the reader has felt a similar benefit. Here are our final suggestions.

It is often helpful to think of children as novices: they frequently face the type of situation we encounter when we take on a new job, start a new relationship, move to a new town, or travel in a foreign country. We can draw upon our own experiences—at any age—to emphathise with their position.

Secondly, it is wise to remember that children do have less power than adults. Parents, teachers and other adults are often children's gatekeepers. They 'make' children do some things, and 'let' them do others. They hold the keys and control the access routes. With no power to change the system, children must use the options open to them. They can express the hope that an adult 'will be a person, not a policeman' or will 'only use power when it's necessary'. They can also become ardent negotiators concerning the details of how the system should work or what the rules should be. The next time we find ourselves a little irritated with their concern about 'fairness', we might remember that it is only the details that they can work on. They cannot leave home or school. They cannot go on strike (except mentally). They can seldom argue safely that parents or teachers have no right to control them. In the face of such differences in power, we might well soften our own use of it, respect their need to have some input, and take seriously their suggestions, not for the abdication of adult power but for its reasonable and shared used.

If you were asked what was pleasant about being with children or irritating about your workday, chances are that the things which come to mind are small and specific events: the way a child looks when asleep, a small gift, some unrequested help, the noise of a colleague, someone borrowing your pens without asking, or being given late notice of something you should have been informed about earlier in the day. Children are no different. It is the small and specific things that matter: 'You can't get a drink when you're thirsty'; 'You can't talk to friends'; 'He said, Goodbye Joanna'. Again and again, these types of events and observations are mentioned as making or breaking the day. Remembering this sense of priorities can also help us to understand children's perspectives.

Finally, we should not forget the significance of adults to children. Children in primary school clearly feel vulnerable. Most of them have an image of adults as providing the essential key to children growing up safe, happy, and competent. Without parents, they say, you would be 'dead' or 'in trouble'. Without teachers, you would grow up 'dumb' and 'couldn't get a job'. Friends may provide the spice of life, but adults are lifelines. That faith is both touching and troubling. Paying attention to the child's-eye view of the world is one step towards living up to it.

NOTES

Introduction: towards a new perception

1   P. Aries *Concepts of Childhood* London: Jonathan Cape, 1962. Australian material expressing this idea may be found in A. Burns and J. J. Goodnow *Children and Families in Australia* Sydney: George Allen & Unwin, 1978.

2   A. L. Brown 'The Development of Memory: Knowing, Knowing about Knowing, and Knowing How to Know' in H. W. Reese (ed.) *Advances in Child Development and Behavior*, vol 10, New York: Academic Press, 1975; and M. T. H. Chi 'Knowledge Structures and Memory Development' in R. S. Siegler (ed.) *Children's Thinking: What Develops?*, Hillsdale N.J.: Erlbaum, 1978.

3   U. Bronfenbrenner *The Ecology of Human Development: Experiments of Nature and Design* Cambridge, Mass: Harvard University Press, 1979. See also Bronfenbrenner 'Ecology of Childhood' in *School Psychology Review* 4, 1980, pp. 294-7, or Bronfenbrenner 'Towards an Experimental Ecology of Human Development' in *American Psychologist* 32, 1977, pp. 513-31.

Chapter 1   Life at home: people

1   The classic examination of this characteristic is by W. J. Livesley and D. B. Bromley *Person Perception in Childhood and Adolescence* London: Wiley, 1973. See also D. G. Perry and K. Bussey *Social Development* Englewood Cliffs, N.J.: Prentice-Hall, 1984.

2   M. Siegal *The Concept of Fairness* New York: Academic Press, 1982.

3   For American material see M. E. Lamb *The Role of the Father in Child Development* New York: Wiley, 1981. For Australian material see G. Russell *The Changing Role of Fathers?* Brisbane: Queensland University Press, 1983.

4   L. Riach 'Me in My Family: A Comparative Study of Young Children's Descriptions of Their Intra-family Interactions' in *Proceedings of National Family Research Conference* vol. 6, Melbourne: Institute of Family Studies, 1984.

5   D. M. Wegner and R. R. Vallacher *Implicit Psychology: An Introduction to Social Cognition* New York: Oxford University Press, 1977. See also Perry and Bussey *Social Development* Englewood Cliffs, N.J.: Prentice-Hall, 1984.
6   J. Dunn and C. Kendrick *Siblings: Love, Envy and Understanding* London: Grant McIntyre, 1982.

Chapter 2   Life at home: activities

1   For a general account see D. G. Perry and K. Bussey *Social Development* Englewood Cliffs, N.J.: Prentice-Hall, 1984.
2   K. Nelson 'Social Cognition in a Script Framework' in J. Flavell and L. Ross *Social Cognitive Development* Cambridge: Cambridge University Press, 1981.
3   J. S. Bruner *Child's Talk* New York: Norton, 1983.
4   U. Bronfenbrenner *The Ecology of Human Development* Cambridge: Harvard University Press, 1977.

Chapter 3   Life at school: teachers

1   B. Davies 'An analysis of Primary School Children's Accounts of Classroom Interaction' in *British Journal of Sociology of Education* 3, 1980, pp. 257-78. See also *Life in the Classroom and Playground: The Accounts of Primary School Children* London: Routledge and Kegan Paul, 1982; J. I. Goodlad *A Place Called School: Prospects for the Future* New York: McGraw-Hill, 1983; and P. Marsh, E. Rosser and R. Harre *The Rules of Disorder* London: Routledge and Kegan Paul, 1978.
2   D. g. Perry and K. Bussey *Social Development* Englewood Cliffs, N.J.: Prentice-Hall, 1984.
3   M. Siegal *The Concept of Fairness* New York: Academic Press, 1982.

Chapter 4   Life at school: activities

1   J. S. Bruner 'On Cognitive Growth' in J. S. Bruner, R. R. Olver and P. H. Greenfield *Studies in Cognitive Growth* New York: Wiley, 1966. See also M. Donaldson *Children's Minds* London: Fontana, 1978.
2   K. Connolly and J. S. Bruner 'Competence: Its Nature and Nurture' in K. Connolly and J. S. Bruner (eds) *The Growth of Competence* New York: Academic Press, 1974.
3   J. I. Goodlad *A Place Called School* New York: McGraw-Hill, 1983; and H. Mehan *Learning Lessons: Social Organizations in the Classrooms* Cambridge, Mass: Harvard University Press, 1979.

Chapter 5 Friends: a special relationship

1 Z. Rubin *Children's Friendships* Cambridge, Mass: Harvard University Press, 1980; and R. L. Selman 'The Child as a Friendship Philosopher' in S. R. Asher and J. M. Gottman (eds) *The Development of Children's Friendships* Cambridge: Cambridge University Press, 1980.
2 V. L. Allen 'Self, Social Group and Social Structure: Surmises about the Study of Children's Friendships' in S. R. Asher and J. M. Gottman (eds) *The Development of Children's Friendships* Cambridge: Cambridge University Press, 1980.
3 S. W. Duck (ed.) *Theory and Practice in Interpersonal Attraction* London: Academic Press, 1977.
4 M. J. Rodin 'Non-engagement, Failure to Engage and Disengagement' in S. W. Duck (ed.) *Personal Relationships Vol. 4: Dissolving Personal Relationships* London: Academic Press, 1982.
5 M. Putallaz and J. M. Gottman 'Social Skills and Group Acceptance' in S. R. Asher and J. M. Gottman (eds) *The Development of Children's Friendships* Cambridge: Cambridge University Press, 1981.
6 J. M. Gottman 'How Children Become Friends' in *Monographs of the Society for Research in Child Development* 48, 1983, no. 201.

Chapter 6 Some guidelines for change

1 U. Bronfenbrenner *The Ecology of Human Development* Cambridge, Mass: Harvard University Press, 1979.
2 H. S. Maas *People and Contexts: Social Development from Birth to Old Age* Englewood Cliff, N.J.: Prentice-Hall, 1984.
3 J. Grusec, *From personal communication with authors*.
4 P. Berger *Facing up to Modernity* Harmondsworth: Penguin, 1977.
5 J. Dunn and C. Kendrick *Siblings: Love, Envy and Understanding* London: Grant McIntyre, 1982.
6 U. Bronfenbrenner *The Ecology of Human Development* Cambridge, Mass: Harvard University Press, 1979.
7 M. Donaldson *Children's Minds* London: Fontana, 1978.
8 M. Poole *Youth in Transition* London: Routledge and Kegan Paul, 1983.
9 B. Davies 'The Role Pupils Play in the Social Construction of Classroom Order' in *British Journal of the Sociology of Education* 4, 1983, pp. 55–69.
10 H. Mehan *Learning Lessons: Social Organization the Classroom* Cambridge, Mass: Cambridge University Press, 1979.

INDEX